AMERICA'S ROAD

A PHOTOGRAPHIC JOURNEY ACROSS THE NATIONAL ROAD FROM BALTIMORE TO EAST ST. LOUIS

RUSSELL C. POOLE

Russell C. Poole

PHOENIX IMAGERY PRESS, LLC

Frederick, Maryland

AMERICA'S ROAD
A photographic journey across
The National Road
from Baltimore to East St. Louis

by Russell C. Poole

Published by :
Phoenix Imagery Press, LLC
415 Shannon Court
Frederick, Maryland 21701
e-mail : info@phoeniximagerypress.com

FIRST EDITION
Copyright © 2006 by Russell C. Poole

Edited by :
Mary R. Brandt
Cynthia A. Poole

Printed in the United States of America

ISBN 0-9770994-0-7

LIBRARY OF CONGRESS CONTROL NUMBER 2005905694

Acknowledgments :

I would like to thank the following people for the encouragement and the valuable input they provided during the course of this project :

Mindy Bianca, John Fieseler, Dan Bonenberger, Deb Keddie, Richard & Jackie Langton, Dennis Baughman, Trish Morgan, Trish & Bill Eccles, Tom Carnegie, Deb & Paul Slater, Michael Bonne, Jerry Roll, Belinda Nickles, Sally Burton, Mary R. Brandt, Cynthia A. Poole, Mary Truitt, Tim Myers, Charles Osgood - for being an inspiration and for his kind words of encouragement, William F. Moran, Jr. - for his creativity and proving you can do the work you love, Norene Halvonik, Donna Holdorf, Roger Anderson, Richard Warmuth, Alan King and the Zane Grey / National Road Museum, Sue Douglass, Will Meadors, Alina Butler, Donna Tauber, Betsy VanHeyde, Joseph Jarzen, Nancy Sartain, Ron Young, Walt Prosser, The Kensington- Algonquin Center staff - Cumberland MD, Janet Davis, Pat Sweitzer, Cindi Ptak, Marci Ross, Glenn Harper, Gabe Hays, and most importantly - to all the wonderful people I've met along the National Road, please know that your suggestions and input were just as important.

In Memoriam :

Carolyn Cook   Resident of the Cumberland, Maryland area
Former editor of German Life Magazine, LaVale, Maryland.
A friend who believed in and supported the efforts of this project
A friend of the National Road

Jerry Hartgrove   Resident of Dunreith, Indiana.
Member of the Board of Directors, Indiana National Road Association
     & a member of the Antique Auto Tour Committee
Volunteer Fire Chief - Dunreith, Indiana
A friend of the National Road

ABOUT THIS BOOK :

The National Road, America's Road, the names provide a hint as to the significance of this relatively short section of highway. From conception as an act of an early Congress, to the realization of the road by the signature of President Thomas Jefferson in 1806, to the long process of construction through a six state wilderness the National Road embodied the dreams of a young nation.

The coming of the National Road allowed for the westward expansion of the nation by any American willing to make the venture, not just the few hardy pioneers who had blazed trails into previously unknown and hostile territory. More importantly the 1806 authorization of the National Road set the stage for the young nation's exploration and settlement of the Northwest Territory, recently acquired through the Treaty of Paris in 1783. The area of the Northwest Territory is now occupied by the states of Illinois, Indiana, Ohio, Michigan, a portion of Minnesota, and Wisconsin. Originally running from the Zero Mile Marker in downtown Cumberland, MD, to the southwest corner of the State House in Vandalia, IL, it is the only highway to ever have been fully funded by the Federal Government. Because of this the National Road holds a unique place in the history of the United States even without the historical events that took place along the route or the famous people who called the route their home.

On June 13, 2002, nearly 200 years after Thomas Jefferson signed the bill approving construction of the National Road the highway received the highest status awarded to a highway, the designation of ALL AMERICAN ROAD. During a ceremony held in Washington, D.C. Mr. Norman Y. Mineta, the U.S. Secretary of Transportation, announced the honor. To receive this status a road must qualify as "a destination unto itself". During April 2006 the National Road will begin a third century of use and the six states through which the National Road runs will host events to celebrate this monumental feat.

The book you now hold in your hands is the culmination of numerous trips over the National Road during a six year period. The text in each section is intended to provide a context and general accompaniment to the images, not a detailed history of the National Road, as many others have already done an excellent job of that task. Instead, my purpose is to show the route as you might see it today by starting at the eastern end and driving continuously until you reach the Mississippi River.

Time has seen many changes to the sights along the route, even within the few years represented here. Some of the historic sites and viewsheds have changed drastically or disappeared entirely in the short time between the last photograph taken and the printing of this book. Because of this it is my sincere hope the pages you are about to view will make you want to get out and see this unique piece of American history for yourself and make you familiar enough with the National Road that you might wish to get involved in saving the wealth of history here before it is gone.

While every effort has been made to ensure the accuracy of the text included in this book along with the captions explaining the photographs, it does not presume to be the definitive work about the National Road. Instead, this book has been created as a personal view that reflects the National Road as seen through my eyes and the lens of my cameras during the many trips to the various sections of the National Road. This book shows that much remains to inspire you, the reader, to take a personal trip along some or all of the road. I feel strongly that anyone making this journey will have a new found admiration for the generations of Americans who preceded us along this route and I hope you will share my enthusiasm and join in the efforts to preserve and maintain this, America's Road.

Russ Poole
Frederick, Maryland

Dedicated to the people of the National Road - past, present, and future.

MARYLAND

A note to visitors - Maryland conducts a National Road Festival during May of each year. The event includes a horse-drawn wagon train traveling from Grantsville to the outskirts of Boonsboro, Maryland. The wagons make regular stops at many points of interest as they wind their way through towns and countryside. Of particular interest is the stop at the Wilson General Store west of Hagerstown. Seeing the wagons cross the historic, five-arch Wilson Bridge takes you back in time. A number of towns along the route have special events during this time to commemorate National Road history.

THE BANK ROAD

The National Road officially began in 1806 at the Zero Mile point along Wills Creek in downtown Cumberland, MD. The names Bank Road, Baltimore Pike, Frederick Road, Frederick Pike, and Cumberland Road were used interchangeably to describe the route stretching from Baltimore, MD to the Zero Mile Marker in Cumberland.

This section is commonly accepted and included as part of the current day National Road. It was created through the efforts of Bankers and Merchants of Baltimore and other towns along the route in an effort to ensure their likely benefit from the planned trade with the West.

The 1806 Congressional authorization of a National Road beginning in Cumberland, Maryland, created a wave of concern between the bankers and merchants in Baltimore City, MD. Fearful that they might miss trade and commerce opportunities opening into the Northwest territories, a decision was made to connect with the National Road at its starting point in Cumberland, Maryland. At the time, Baltimore City was a rapidly growing seaport and industrial base. It was particularly concerned with the possible loss of trade and the impact it would have on the city. The connection with the National Road's starting point in Cumberland was viewed as another source of revenue from the distribution of goods being produced by the growing city.

Their goal was accomplished through the consolidation and extension of the numerous public roads and privately held toll roads throughout the region. Each section was connected to form a continuous "pike" to transport goods to Cumberland. Many smaller roads began as a means for the larger farms to transport their crops to mills to be ground for flour and feed or to transport tobacco crops to the port for shipment overseas. Examples of this system were the roads from the B&O Railroad terminal at Ellicott City to the Charles Carroll Farm at Doureghan Manor and the Frederick to Walkersville Toll Road which brought crops and goods from the north-central part of Frederick County to the railroad station and then on to Baltimore for shipment or sale.

A number of crude roads and privately held toll roads were already in existence to connect the farms and estates west of Baltimore to the numerous growing small towns and their services. Examples of these lesser roads would include the Rolling Road, the road to Doureghan Manor, sections of the Frederick to Walkersville Toll Road, and the Frederick Pike heading west.

Rolling Road was used to roll hogsheads of tobacco, large barrels weighing several hundred pounds each, to ships waiting at the port of Elkridge, Maryland. The road to Doureghan Manor connected the farm to the Ellicott Brothers grain mills at Ellicott City, Maryland.

The Frederick to Walkersville Toll Road entered the outskirts of Frederick connecting it to the National Road at the Monocacy River and ran north to Walkersville, eventually continuing on into the northern section of Frederick County.

The Frederick Pike, now the National Road through Frederick, carried passengers and goods west to Hagerstown and the other population centers growing throughout western Maryland. This network of roads created the logical opportunity for consolidation into a single, passable road in order to create the continuous passageway necessary to connect the Baltimore Harbor with the National Road at Cumberland, Maryland. This effort provided the basic infrastructure which later would become known as the National Pike, the Bank Road, the Frederick Road, or the Cumberland Road depending on the section traveled.

The travelers' need for points of reference was handled uniquely by the creation of carved stone "mile markers." A simple flat faced marker with a rounded top, looking much like a small gravestone, was created of stone quarried locally near the site. One of these markers was then placed on the north side of the road at the start of each mile. The system of marking began in downtown Baltimore, not far from the harbor. A simple carved inscription of "B" above the inscription "(number) M" told the distance in miles from that location to or from Baltimore while heading east or west.

Upon reaching downtown Cumberland, the stone mile markers ended. At the original starting location of the National Road, a single stone marker was placed denoting the spot as the "Zero Mile." All markers from that point west to the Maryland and Pennsylvania border were made of cast iron, painted white, and were again placed only on the north side of the road. Each marker carried the miles to Cumberland, MD cast into the southeastern face and the miles to the next city or town cast into the southwestern face. This method of marking was easily seen and provided the wagons, drovers, and other travelers with more detailed information useful for planning their rest and overnight stops.

BALTIMORE

The city of Baltimore (founded 1729) was a well known and firmly established port of trade prior to the coming of the National Road in the early 1800s.

Nearby is Fort McHenry known for the battle fought there in 1814 which inspired a young Frederick lawyer, Francis Scott Key, to pen the words to the Star Spangled Banner. Fort McHenry is the only site in the National Park System to be designated as both a National Monument and a Historic Shrine.

The Bank Road, or National Road as we know it today, begins in downtown Baltimore City, Maryland near the Baltimore Harbor. It then proceeds west, passing through the area known as West End, and on into Baltimore County and the small-town of Irvington. From there, we will follow the road as it moves into Catonsville, Maryland and continue west until crossing the Patapsco River where it leaves Baltimore County.

The National Road travels west on city streets past the B&O railroad bridge near West Side and on toward the suburb of Irvington. Both the railroads and the localized trolley lines were popular early forms of transportation though little remains now to indicate their importance in early Baltimore history.

Mitchell Court House - Baltimore, Maryland

Left - A view of the Fort McHenry courtyard from a barracks window

Below - Another view of the Fort McHenry Courtyard as seen from the southeast rampart wall. A replica of the original Star Spangled Banner flies overhead.

Entrance to Loudon Park Cemetery - Irvington, Maryland

Approaching Irvington, the National Road passes alongside a section of historic Loudon Park Cemetery, now known as the Loudon National Cemetery. Dating to the mid 1800s, Loudon Park contains the remains of more than two thousand Union soldiers buried amid the grounds.

The cemetery also contains the burial sites of Mary Pickersgill, the seamstress who created the original Star Spangled Banner, and the legendary Baltimore writer and curmudgeon, H.L. Mencken.

A short distance ahead, the National Road enters Irvington. Once a distant and affluent suburb of Baltimore, the area today shows signs of urban decay intermixed with buildings undergoing restoration and renovation.

Evidence of the trolley tracks that ran between here and downtown Baltimore until the late 1950s can still be found.
The most impressive site along this section of road is the Mt. St. Joseph High School. A short distance beyond the school in the front yard of a local church to our right, stands an original, carved-stone National Road mile marker.

Leaving the Irvington area, the road continues up a grade past a National Military Cemetery to the area known as Paradise Junction. A short distance beyond this point is the beginning of Catonsville, Maryland.

Crossing the bridge over the modern day Baltimore Beltway we reach Catonsville and pass a combination gas station and convenience store on the right. Standing in front of the building at the roadside is a stone mile marker and next to it a metal historic plaque. The plaque tells us that this is the Six Mile Marker which indicates we have traveled six miles from downtown Baltimore. Since six miles of travel up and down grades by horse drawn wagons was a trip requiring the major part of a day, the town of Catonsville became a popular stopping point. Allowing horses to water and rest or providing overnight lodging in local inns, the town quickly grew as a result of the National Road - here known as the Frederick Pike.

At the western end of town, the road passes Rolling Road on the right. Used as a path to roll large hogsheads (similar to a barrel or cask) of tobacco, weighing several hundred pounds, to the port of Elkridge for shipment to Europe, it was important to the local farming communities.

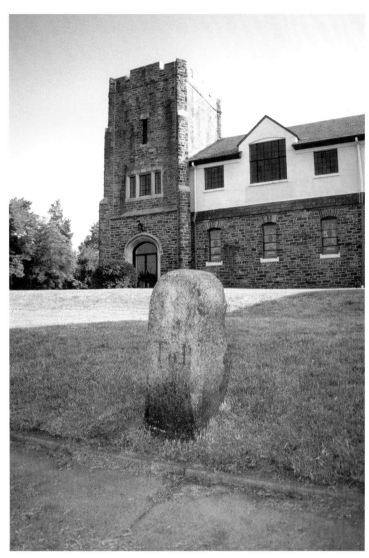

Left - An original National Road mile marker stands along the sidewalk in front of a west Baltimore church

Right - The "six mile" marker and a placard describing it stand in front of a convenience store and gas station along Frederick Road - The National Road - at Catonsville, Maryland

From here the National Road runs approximately five miles before descending a steep grade into the Patapsco River Valley and the town of Ellicott City, home to the Ellicott Brothers Mills.

ELLICOTT CITY

Originally called Ellicott Mills after the founding Ellicott Brothers, this site was chosen for the second location of the mills after a previous unsuccessful attempt to the north. The original mill, previously known as Upper Ellicott Mills was located along the Patapsco River a few miles north of the present site in an area now known as Daniels, Maryland.

The Baltimore & Ohio Railroad Station - Ellicott City, Maryland

Immediately upon crossing the Patapsco River and entering the lower end of Ellicott City, the traveler passes under a railroad bridge and can see the stone Baltimore & Ohio Railroad Station to the left and a stone mile marker, embedded in the brick sidewalk, to the right.

It was here during the summer of 1830 that the famous locomotive the Tom Thumb made its initial run, a trip from Baltimore to the Ellicott City station. Designed by New Yorker Peter Cooper, it was the most powerful steam locomotive of the time. During August of 1830, the Tom Thumb raced against a horse drawn carriage to prove the superiority of the modern train. Though the Tom Thumb developed a significant lead, a broken drive belt caused defeat much to the delight of those favoring the horse. Aside from this loss, the small locomotive demonstrated the utility of rail transportation. It foreshadowed the coming competition and ultimate victory over the National Road as the railroads provided a faster and more efficient means of trade with the west.

As the National Road continues into the heart of town it becomes the main street of Ellicott City. The town is made up of many unique craft shops, artisan studios, antique shops, and other small businesses. Restaurants now fill storefronts which earlier housed lumber companies, clothing stores, cobbler's shops and the local newspaper offices.

The hillsides surrounding the town are home to local historic sites including the Patapsco Female Institute. Unusual for the early 1800s, it was an elite private boarding school for young women of aristocratic southern families.

Above - an interpretive placard stands in front of the Thomas Isaac Cabin at Ellicott City, MD.

Left - The Thomas Isaac Cabin c. 1780

At the upper end of Main Street we find the Thomas Isaac Cabin, a relocated and restored log building. The cabin has now been stocked with period items and is used to depict an early stage stop during the infancy of the National Road.

Nearby and on the opposite side of the street stands a mid 1900s service station, now in use as an office. Located on a hillside above the street is the Colored School House, an early 1900s one room school currently in the process of being renovated to accurately show its former use. Renovations may be completed by the time the 200th Anniversary of the National Road is celebrated during 2006.

From here the National Road continues the journey through the western end of Ellicott City, past rows of smaller joined houses built during the early and mid 1900s.

Above - The B&O Railroad Station at Ellicott City, MD.

Left - Lower end of Main Street - Ellicott City, MD

Below - A National Road mile marker embedded in the sidewalk beneath the B&O Railroad bridge at Ellicott City, MD

Leaving the town behind us, the road reaches an intersection with St. John's Lane. Immediately beyond the intersection is a large stone church and at the side of the road, an original mile marker.

A few miles further, the road passes the manor houses of Grey Rock and then Font Hill Manor. Both were originally part of the land holdings of Charles Carroll, a signer of the Declaration of Independence.

At this point the road reaches an abrupt end forcing us to travel across the modern day Maryland Route 40. Just before making the turn in the road to join Route 40, we can see a trace of the old roadbed along with a remaining mile marker. This short piece of the original road now serves as access to a private residence.

Once on westbound Route 40, we travel the left lane for approximately a half-mile before bearing left to return to the original National Road course on what is now known as, Maryland Route 144. While descending a slight grade we can see a long stretch of split rail fence and farmland to the left. This is the northern boundary of Doureghan Manor, once the home of Charles Carroll of Carrollton, the longest surviving signer of the Declaration of Independence. Though the farm has dwindled to slightly more than eight hundred acres, Doughregan Manor is owned to this day by descendants of Charles Carroll.

Our trip continues past farmland and newer development along this rural road for approximately eight miles until reaching an intersection with Maryland Route 32 at the small town of West Friendship Maryland. The town is little more than a crossroads with a small shopping center and scattered residences on the surrounding lands.

Crossing Route 32 the National Road proceeds west for approximately eight to ten miles as a two-lane rural road. The intersection with Maryland Route 97 marks the small town of Cooksville, Maryland which remains quiet since the heyday of the National Road. Crossing Route 97, we continue our journey westward.

The next town we come to is Lisbon, Maryland, followed by the tiny village of Poplar Springs. Today both are seen as a cluster of small homes along the road.

During the early days of the National Road, Poplar Springs was an important stopping point for travelers who replenished their water supplies at the local spring for which the town was named. Today it is somewhat difficult to find the original location of the spring unless carefully watching for the sign.

As we reach the western end of Howard County, we enter the town of Mount Airy which is situated in the area known as "four counties". With the intersecting borders of Howard, Carroll, Frederick and Montgomery counties and bypassed by the Interstate highway, Mount Airy has managed to not only survive but in some ways thrive. A side trip to the downtown area reveals new construction, much renovation, and a revitalization effort with small businesses filling formerly empty storefronts. All this aside, the loss of vehicular traffic, other than that of residents commuting, and the presence of modern super stores at the southern end near the Interstate bodes ill for the future of the town's core.

NEW MARKET

A mile marker at the east end of New Market, MD

Leaving Mount Airy on the National Road we begin to descend into a valley and through the area formerly known as Delaplane or Plane Number 7, before traveling on to the historic town of New Market, Maryland. Plane Number 7 was the site of a number of thriving small businesses and a farm equipment shop until the construction of Interstate 70 bypassed the area during the 1970s. A trip through the area today reveals a car repair shop and a weed choked farm implement store. This is yet another area that struggled unsuccessfully to survive the transition from a busy route to one that sees little travel today.

Coming to the intersection with Maryland Route 75, the National Road crosses and enters New Market from the east end. If we stop and look left after the sharp left turn, a portion of the original road track and a small 1900s Bridge can be seen. The section was filled in to build up the road surface for the modern routing of Route 75. As we continue into New Market, an original stone mile marker can be seen along the right shoulder.

Reaching the center of New Market we find this small town, bypassed by the construction of Interstate Route 70, has reinvented itself into the Antiques Capitol of Maryland. In the process of doing so the town has made a great effort to restore buildings and maintain the charm of an early 20th century town in a manner consistent with what was commonly found along the early National Road.

FREDERICK

Slightly more than four miles ahead, the National Road brings us to the outskirts of the historic city of Frederick, Maryland. The original road bed crossed the Monocacy River on the Jug Bridge, passing an early toll house built for use by the Frederick to Walkersville Toll Road.

The road continues up the grade from the river and passes a park and ride area with an unusual monument at one end. This is the relocated Jug Bridge demi-john, a monument made from local stone and patterned after the wide base and narrow neck shape common to flasks and wicker covered bottles. Erected in honor of a visit to Frederick by Revolutionary War hero General the Marquis de Lafayette during December 1824, the monument stood at the west end of the original bridge across the Monocacy River and caused the local residents to refer to the structure as the Jug Bridge, a name still in use. We now leave the Jug Bridge Monument parking lot and continue to follow the National Road west for a short distance to the edge of the city of Frederick.

In the early 1700s migratory German settlers from Pennsylvania settled in various small villages along the Monocacy river in the area north of modern day Frederick. In the 1730s a portion of a land tract, previously patented by Patrick Dulaney under an offer to encourage settlement in the area, was used to create the city of Fredericktowne. Many of the settlers in the outlying areas would choose to relocate to this new location. Formally founded in 1745, the fast growing city would eventually become known by the present day name of Frederick.

The city has managed to retain much of its local charm with a rich mixture of historic homes, museums, antique shops, restaurants, and houses of worship. The arts thrive with live theater, galleries, community art works, and the Delaplaine Visual Arts Center - an active local art center and gallery. Though Baltimore receives more recognition in the history books, a number of the people and events significant to early Maryland and American history were Frederick related.

The National Museum of Civil War Medicine on east Patrick Street consists of three floors of displays. The displays depict life for the soldiers, Union and Confederate, during the Civil War as well as the medical processes and innovations in use at the time. The Museum site is one of many buildings and churches throughout town that were pressed into use as field hospitals during the Civil War battles of South Mountain and Antietam. Today the Museum frequently hosts re-enactors demonstrating and speaking about the medical practices of the time from battlefield life to surgery or embalming the dead.

A large number of the downtown buildings lining Patrick Street have been in existence since the late 1700s and many of them can be seen in photographs taken at the time of the Civil War. Some of the preserved photographs may be viewed at the National Civil War Museum and the nearby Frederick Historical Society.

A short distance off the National Road, we find the Hessian Barracks built in 1777 to house Hessian mercenaries and captured British soldiers. Many of the prisoners were placed on work details throughout the area and quite a few chose to remain here after they were freed. The building remained a prison until 1782 when it became the first Maryland School for the Deaf.

In 1803 it was a staging point for the Lewis and Clark Expedition. Due to concern that opponents of the expedition in Washington, D.C. might attempt to sabotage the effort, Lewis and Clark had their initial supplies held at the Hessian Barracks.

During the Civil War period, the barracks were used as a field hospital to tend to the many soldiers wounded in nearby battles.

Barbara Fritchie House - Frederick, MD

Further along the National Road / Patrick Street we come to a spot where Carroll Creek crosses under the road and located next to it is a small brick house. This is the Barbara Fritchie House. Destroyed by Hurricane Agnes during the 1970s, the historic home was reconstructed and now serves as a museum.

According to the verses of the poem ***Barbara Fritchie***, written by American poet John Greenleaf Whittier, an elderly Barbara Fritchie is said to have defiantly waved the Stars and Stripes from her upstairs window as Confederate troops passed by on west Patrick Street. The bronze tablet attached to Barbara Fritchie's grave in nearby Mt. Olivet Cemetery has the entire poem engraved upon it. Whittier's poem also mentions the Clustered Spires of Frederick, the five visible spires atop four closely grouped downtown churches. The term ***Clustered Spires*** has since been adopted as a descriptive slogan for the city.

Above - A view of the Hessian Barracks - Frederick, MD

Below - The original Law Office of Francis Scott Key & his brother-in-law Roger Brooke Taney

Above - Downtown Frederick, MD and the Clustered Spires as seen from Carroll Creek in Baker Park

Below - The Shared Vision Bridge Mural - painted to provide the appearance of an ivy covered stone bridge. The Delaplaine Visual Arts Center is in the background. Mural painting on the bridge is © William Cochran

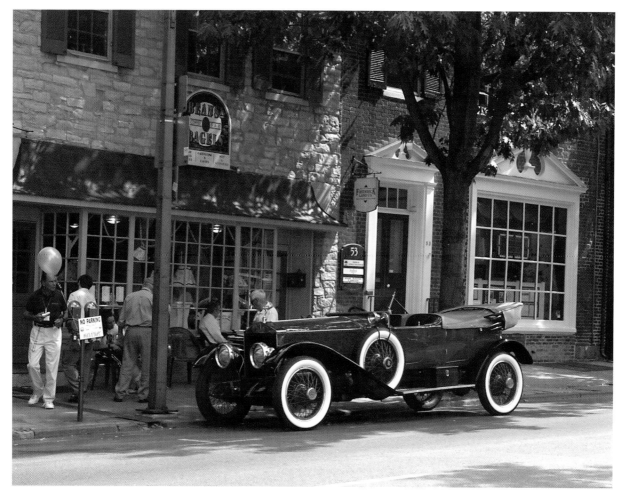

Above - A vintage Rolls Royce stops on the National Road in Frederick, MD during a Rolls Royce Silver Ghost Tour

Below left -An original mile marker stands in front of a downtown business in Frederick, MD

Below right - An american flag hangs from a crane over Baker Park during a 4th of July celebration in Frederick, MD

Not far from the Barbara Fritchie House is the building which once housed the law offices of Francis Scott Key, a Frederick county native, and his brother-in-law Roger Brooke Taney. Jointly operated by these men, the building still stands across from the current day City Hall. Francis Scott Key is best known for writing the Star Spangled Banner while detained on a ship near the battle at Fort McHenry in 1814. Roger Brooke Taney, as Chief Justice of the United States, is best remembered for the infamous Dred Scott Decision which declared slaves to be the personal property of their owners.

Francis Scott Key is buried in nearby Mt. Olivet Cemetery. A chapel and a large statue stand near the site in honor of Key. Other notable Marylanders buried in Mt. Olivet include Thomas Johnson the first Governor of Maryland, and local historic figure Barbara Fritchie. The cemetery also holds the graves of more than four hundred Confederate Soldiers killed during the Civil War at the Battle of the Monocacy which took place a few miles south of Frederick. Though not one of the more widely recognized events, it is credited with being the "battle that saved Washington".

The 1756 Jacob Brunner house, named Schifferstadt in honor of the builder's German home city, is now completely restored and is open as the Schifferstadt Architectural Museum.

One of the oldest and best preserved German houses in America, Schifferstadt offers visitors an opportunity to see first hand how early German settlers lived in the area.

Each October Schifferstadt plays host to an old time Ocktoberfest offering German food and music, crafters, and tours of the museum.

The early 1900s Tivoli Theater, now known as the Weinberg Center for the Arts.

Above left - A view of the relatively plain exterior
Above right - A view of the exterior lobby and gilded ticket booth
Below - A view of the central seating area and the stage

Above & Below - Delphey's - A Frederick, MD landmark . Originally begun during the early 1900s as a Harley Davidson Motorcycle dealer, Delphey's was an important part of the evolving motorized transportation scene developing across the National Road corridor. Located on the National Road, business was so successful it earned a personal visit from William Davidson who had to see for himself the shop that had sold so many of his motorcycles. The repair shop was located in the basement of the building, accessible by a ramp at the rear of the structure, while the showroom faced the road at street level

Despite the historic importance of this facility, the city of Frederick recently demolished the building in order to expand parking for the nearby modern courthouse and to build space for state government offices.

Leaving the summit of South Mountain, the National Road drops abruptly down the western slope through a series of switchback turns until it finally reaches the valley floor and the eastern edge of Washington County.

An interesting side note - Washington County, Maryland was the first county in the United States to be officially named in honor of George Washington.

The area making up the eastern outskirts of Boonsboro, Maryland in Washington County, is also known as the Crossroads of the Civil War. This area literally served as a crossroads of travel for the Union and Confederate troops heading to Antietam or Gettysburg, Monocacy or South Mountain, and any of the lesser skirmishes that took place in this part of the country. Boonsboro, Maryland is a small town located within easy driving range of the sites of numerous major Civil War battles, including the Battle of Antietam and the Battle of South Mountain.

Here again the National Road serves as the main route through the town. As we drive along Main Street note the various buildings from the early 1900s that are renovated to serve modern day needs.

A local point of interest is the Boonsboro Museum, owned and operated by resident and local historian Doug Bast. Situated in front of the Bast family furniture business, the museum houses Mr. Bast's private collection of artifacts from all eras of the town's history and many original Civil War pieces. The museum is open to the public on a limited basis. Another popular spot for visitors to Boonsboro is a local bookstore owned and operated by internationally famous author Nora Roberts and her family. Another popular tourist destination nearby is the Crystal Grotto Caverns, located a few miles south of town.

As we leave the town of Boonsboro, the National Road passes a former stockyard site now in use as a restaurant and flea market. Painted in a patriotic red, white, and blue theme the building now serves as a prominent landmark along the original route of the Bank Road / National Road.

A short distance beyond the stockyard we pass a stone mile marker on the right and then the site of a restored lime kiln located on the left, all of which are reminders of the early days of Washington County, Maryland.

Above left - The Newcomer lime kiln west of Boonsboro, MD
Above right - An original National Road mile marker. This example tells us it is 66 miles to Baltimore
Below - Wagons participating in the annual National Pike Days festivities travel the National Road past the 66 mile marker

HAGERSTOWN

Next along the National Road we enter the small town of Funkstown, Maryland. Originally created as a separate town, Funkstown has now become an outlying section of nearby Hagerstown, Maryland due to the growth of the larger city.

Hagerstown, Maryland, also known as Hub City, was founded in 1762 by Jonathan Hager. The most prominent features of the city are the large number of early 1900s homes and other business buildings remaining. It is quite easy to walk through the old part of town and have a feel for how it might have looked to early National Road travelers.

Hagerstown is divided by Washington Street traveling east and Franklin Street west. These two roads remain a block apart through the city's length. In most towns, the National Road was a single route through the area and allowed travel east and west along a single passage. The practice of creating separate roads for each direction became more pronounced during the early 1900s as State Highway departments attempted to improve the flow of traffic through the cities. This practice will be observed in many of the more populated towns and cities as we continue our journey across the six states through which the National Road runs.

The Hagerstown City Park has been listed by National Geographic as one of the 10 most beautiful places in the United States. The restored Jonathan Hager House is located adjacent to the park and is open to the public.

WILSON GENERAL STORE

A few miles west of Hagerstown we reach the area known as Huyett, now little more than a crossroads with a convenience store and scattered private residences. Notable at this location is a still active Mennonite schoolhouse a short distance past the intersection on the right side of the National Road.

Further along we pass a historic marker proclaiming the road we are traveling as the Bank Road and giving a brief history of the origins of the name.

Continuing our journey the road enters an area known as Wilson, Maryland.

The National Road today crosses the Conococheague River on the present day Route 40, paralleling the original route across the historic Wilson Bridge. The Wilson Bridge, a sturdy and original five-arch stone bridge remaining from the heyday of National Road travel, stands today as a monument to the stonemason's craft.

"THE BANK ROAD"
(THE CUMBERLAND TURNPIKE ROAD)
THE PORTION OF THIS HIGHWAY FROM THE WEST END OF THE CONOCOCHEAGUE BRIDGE TO CUMBERLAND (40 MILES) WAS BUILT BETWEEN 1816 AND 1821. THE BANKS OF MARYLAND FINANCED IT BY PURCHASE OF THE STOCK.
STATE ROADS COMMISSION

The five arch Wilson Bridge as seen from the north side (above) and from the current Route 40 bridge (below) located to the south of the original path of the National Road.

Above - The Wilson General Store and Post Office located west of Hagerstown, MD.

Below - Participants in the annual National Pike Days Festival travel by horseback and covered wagon across the Wilson Bridge on the original National Road.

A small roadside park, accessed just east of the river crossing, allows for exploration of the bridge at a safe distance from the current high speed road. From this point visitors can take a leisurely stroll across the bridge. Each May during the National Pike Festival, a horse drawn wagon train travels from southwest Pennsylvania to the town of Boonsboro usually crossing the original Wilson Bridge while en route.

After exploring the Wilson Bridge on foot, we will proceed to cross the river on the modern Route 40 bridge and turn left in order to travel the original route past the Wilson General Store.

An important site to weary travelers, for rest and supplies, the Wilson General Store (mid 1800s) was transformed into a general community store and Post Office during latter years of use. Now restored and run as a general store and antique mart, the store displays numerous antiques from the beginning days of the National Road through the end of the 20th century.

Displayed outside at the west end of the building are antique farm items and wagons. Located on the property adjacent to the store are two restored buildings, the one-room Wilson schoolhouse (1855) and a small restored chapel.

Leaving Wilson and the General Store we return to Route 40 and continue on our trip west.

CLEAR SPRING

After passing through rolling countryside and open farmland, the National Road comes to the town of Clear Spring, Maryland.

Clear Spring (1821) earned its name from a tiny spring head located near the center of town. The spring was well known as a source of potable water for travelers and originally the main source of water for settlers in the region. A sign along the main street points out the location of the spring, where a short walk along a narrow space between the buildings brings us to the actual location. The spring site, still deceptive in appearance with crystal clear and inviting waters, is well kept. But please be aware of the sign above the spring which states that today the water is no longer fit to drink.

Leaving Clear Spring the National Road begins a steep climb up the mountain, toward the area known as Indian Springs.

Passing through Indian springs, we will descend the western side of the mountain and enter a river valley created by the long time action of the nearby Potomac River.

Located a short distance off the National Road, but well worth the side trip, is historic Fort Frederick.

Built during 1756, the large stone enclosure was prominent in the defense of the Maryland frontier during the French and Indian war. The massive size of the fort can only be experienced by passing through the stout wooden gates and observing the reconstructed barracks and the outlines of numerous other barracks that once stood inside these walls. In later years Fort Frederick served as a prison for Hessian and British soldiers during the American Revolution.

Leaving Fort Frederick behind we return to the National Road.

The road once again continues west until we are forced to merge onto Interstate 70 due to the modern Interstate being built on top of the original National Road route in this area. Our trip will now follow Route 70 for a few miles until we exit to return to the National Road at the riverside town of Hancock, Maryland.

HANCOCK

Hancock, Maryland, seated in a fertile valley of the Potomac River, was first settled in the early 1700s.

A toll house once operated by a private toll road company west of Hancock, MD

At the western end of Washington County, Hancock has evolved into a major orchard center for Maryland and produces more apples and other tree fruit than any area of the state except northern Frederick County.

Hancock is also home to the Chesapeake & Ohio (C&O) Canal headquarters and information center. The information center is easily reached by making a left turn on the National Road at the bottom of the exit ramp.

The narrow streets of Hancock have recently been rebuilt. Though incorporating modern technology and methods, the streets appear much like they were throughout the 1900s giving the town a friendly small town appeal.

Leaving Hancock, the National Road begins a casual ascent and passes a toll house from the era of privately held toll roads, in operation long before the National Road was built. The building, recently renovated, gives the visitor a glimpse of both the isolated life and cramped quarters of the toll master and his family during the early 1800s.

With the town behind us, the National Road begins the steepest ascent yet encountered as it begins the rolling climb up Sideling Hill toward the area known as Little Orleans.

The National Road winds into a valley west of Hancock while the current Interstate 70 passes through the Sidling Hill cut in the distance.

Nearing the top of the mountain, we reach an extreme curve, commonly referred to as a horseshoe curve due to the tightly curved shape, complete with warning lights at the top.

The lights and warning signs were installed during the early 1900s to warn motorists of the severity of the curve and prevent vehicles from running straight into the mountainside ahead.

Looking east at the horseshoe curve on the National Road near the summit of Sidling Hill

Proceeding to the top of the next mountain we encounter the Town Hill Hotel. Constructed in the early 1900s it was the first hotel in Maryland built specifically to cater to the newly created automobile trade that came to the National Road. The placement of the hotel at the top of such a steep grade allowed early automobile travelers to refill their radiators and allow their engines and transmissions to cool before descending the severe western grade toward the town of Flintstone, Maryland or the equally severe grade of the eastern slope towards the Baltimore and Washington area.

Now under new ownership and recently renovated, the Town Hill Hotel features dining, lodging, and a breathtaking view from an overlook opposite the main building.

We now leave the summit and descend Town Hill toward our next stop, the town of Flintstone, Maryland.

FLINTSTONE

The Flintstone Hotel

Travelers surviving the white knuckle ride downhill from the Town Hill Hotel will enter into yet another valley before continuing the drive to Flintstone, Maryland.

An antique interior latch from the Flintstone Hotel

Entering Flintstone we pass a school with a historic marker in front. The marker describes this section of the National Road as an original part of the Warrior's Path. The Warrior's Path is the longest major Indian trail known and stretches from central New York State, passing through Flintstone Gap, to the eastern mountains of the Carolinas.

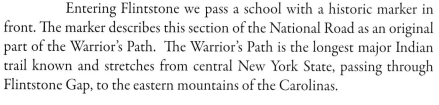

Passing the school we encounter on the right a large building with multiple chimneys. This is the Flintstone Hotel, built in 1807, which thrived on the business of the many travelers passing by on what was then the only main route west.

An old sign found in the attic at the Flintstone Hotel

The west end view of the Flintstone Hotel gives a more accurate representation of the structure's enormous size.

Owners Richard and Jackie Langton, a descendant of the original builders, reside here and are working on the restoration of the hotel with the goal of creating a unique Bed and Breakfast along with a showcase for local history when the task is completed.

The remainder of Flintstone is reminiscent of the typical small town encountered along the National Road, consisting of a gas station with combined store, numerous well-kept private residences, a neighborhood tavern, and local churches of various denominations.

Leaving Flintstone we again encounter a steep upward grade that leads us across the crest of the next mountain before descending to a short side trip to Rocky Gap State Park.

Rocky Gap park was built around man-made Lake Habeeb and features a modern hotel, restaurant and conference center, golf course, campgrounds, in addition to the recreational lake. The improvements were planned as an economic boost for Allegany County and nearby Cumberland, Maryland with the hope of replacing some of the jobs and revenue lost when major businesses relocated away from the once thriving industrial town.

Crossing back over top of Route 70, the road continues the descent and passes an older white painted building on the left with a sign telling us it is the Rocky Gap Gift Shop.

The building was originally known as the 8 Mile House, a roadside tavern and restaurant. Previously deserted and offered for sale for many years, the overgrowth of weeds and brush are now cleared. Completely renovated and saved from demolition, the building remains largely unchanged in appearance from the mid 1900s except for the removal of two chimneys, one at each end, and a porch area added on during the 1970s.

A short distance further along we pass a small residential area of early to mid 1900s houses situated quite close to the path of the original road. Across the road is a 1900s church, saved only by the route of Interstate 70 curving around the back of it, but losing most of the church property. The church cemetery is located directly across the National Road.

Traveling another mile of the road brings us past yet another older residential area consisting of a few houses located at the roadside and a small gas station. Buildings that used to house businesses in this area are mostly vacant as is a roadside motel. Ahead a recently built intersection with a modernized Route 220 heads north toward Bedford, Pennsylvania. Most vehicles traveling the Interstate exit only to travel only as far as the Route 220 intersection or they continue east on Route 70 bypassing the old road and leaving this area to deteriorate.

The road now approaches the outskirts of Cumberland, Maryland, the site of the official beginning of the National Road.

CUMBERLAND

Cumberland, Maryland was founded in the mid 1700s when land in the area was purchased from the local Indians.

As we enter Cumberland the National Road becomes known as Baltimore Street and flows into the downtown business area near the restored and still operating Western Maryland Railroad Station. With numerous points of interest and ample parking at both the Railroad Station and the nearby Canal Place, the site is worth taking time to visit. Outside, centered in a stone and brick courtyard, stands a sculpture of a mule and young boy, symbols of early days of the C&O (Chesapeake & Ohio) Canal. The sculpture was created by Frederick County, Maryland artist Toby Mendez.

The adjacent Canal Place hosts numerous shops and eateries with an early Canal Boat on permanent display nearby.

Behind the Railroad Station is a new pedestrian bridge over Wills Creek which leads to the George Washington Cabin site. The bridge can be reached after a short walk from the parking lot and can be seen from the loading platform of the station.

Inside the upper level of the massive station we find the ticket counter for locomotive trips on a unique, steam train trip to Frostburg. The polished metal and finely finished wood found within the station are reminders of the glory days of passenger railroads.

Located at the ground level, with an entrance at the side of the building, are the National Park Service C&O Canal information center and museum.

The steam train prepares to leave the station at Cumberland for the round trip journey through the mountains to Frostburg, MD.

Above - The Western MD Train Station at Cumberland, MD. Foreground sculpture © Toby Mendez

Below - A historical marker located along the current day route of the National Road through The Narrows at Cumberland, MD

We have now reached the end of our trip across the Bank Road from Baltimore to Cumberland, Maryland. We will travel across Wills Creek to the original starting point of the National Road, located at the Zero Mile Marker in downtown Cumberland.

THE NATIONAL ROAD

The National Road had its official beginning in 1806 at the Zero Mile marker along the banks of Wills Creek in downtown Cumberland, Maryland.

Though now accepted as part of the National Road, the names Bank Road, Frederick Road, Frederick Pike, or Cumberland Road are used only to identify the section of the road east of Cumberland stretching from downtown Baltimore, Maryland to the Zero Mile marker in Cumberland.

The Zero Mile marker indicates the actual starting point of the National Road as it was designated by Congress and signed into being by President Thomas Jefferson in early 1806. This marker originally sat along the banks of Wills Creek near the current day location of George Washington's headquarters but was moved to a location about fifty yards west during the early 1900s to allow for road construction.

On a hill overlooking the marker and Washington's headquarters stands the Emmanuel Episcopal Church. The present day church is built atop the original 1755 location of Fort Cumberland. It was here that a young George Washington received his first military commission and later surrendered his last commission from military service. Tunnels that ran beneath the fort still remain and are open for visitors to tour during Cumberland's annual Heritage Days and other special events.

Through the early 1900s, as Route 28 was created and moved into West Virginia, the zero mile marker was relocated to allow re-routing of the road. The marker was placed in the center island of Route 28 at the foot of Green Street.

Known originally as the Braddock Road, Green Street proceeds from the creek valley at the foot of Fort Cumberland up and across part of Haystack Mountain. It continues west before descending into the area now known as LaVale, Maryland.

PENNSYLVANIA

Leaving Maryland and traveling up the grade into Pennsylvania we see two signs on the north shoulder of the road. The larger blue sign gives information about the National Road in Pennsylvania while the smaller sign displays a red, white and blue shield and the words Historic National Road.

From this point west through the remaining five states in the National Road Corridor this sign will be your guide. Each of these states chose to display the shield either alone or with a graphic in the center showing a particular aspect of their state. The road signs include the words Historic National Road to denote the route. The intent is to create continuity no matter where the traveler joins the route and to allow the road to be followed easily. The signs are highly visible and installation has been completed throughout most of the remaining miles of the National Road.

ADDISON

Here the original road splits off to the left, while the current day Route 40 continues straight ahead. Turning to follow the original route we travel up a small grade to enter the town of Addison, Pennsylvania.

The most striking structure in Addison is an excellent example of the early toll houses built along the National Road. This particular building is constructed of large blocks of light brown sandstone. All of the toll houses originally built along the National Road share this same design.

As seen previously in the LaVale, Maryland toll house, the room at the top front of the building was the toll masters bedroom and the multiple windows allowed him a complete view of the night time traffic on the road by simply sitting up in bed. Fortunately, the existing current road follows the original road track making this easier to visualize.

In common with the other two toll houses along the route, the Addison Toll house is periodically opened to the public.

When the National Pike festival is held during early May of each year the toll house serves as a stopping point for the wagon train.

This toll house displays many period items and furniture that would have been used by a family residing here in the early 1800s. A unique feature in this example is a small access door off the stairwell near the main bedroom. This was used as a sleeping loft by the toll master's numerous children.

As you visit the site, take time to observe the cast iron gate posts located across the road at the entrance to a small park.

Originally, one post on each side of the road held a barrier which was swung across the road to bar passage until the traveler met with the toll master and the necessary fee was paid.

Outside of the toll house is a large stone slab with a bronze plaque attached to it. Note that the plaque tells about the Great Crossings Bridge, though it seems out of place here. A few miles from this spot we will again encounter the name Great Crossings as we reach the Youghiogheny River. During periods of extremely low water levels we may even see the remains of the bridge to which this plaque was originally attached.

Above & below - interior furnishings typical of the early days of the National Road.
The Addison Toll House - Addison, PA.

SOMERVILLE - GREAT CROSSING

Leaving the town of Addison, the National Road runs over gently rolling terrain until returning to the current highway a few miles west of town and beginning a long descent towards the Youghiogheny River Reservoir.

The lake ahead was created during the early 1900s when the river was dammed. The flooded steep valley covered both the original Great Crossings Bridge and the then existing town of Somerville, Pennsylvania.

A right turn into the park area at the east end of the bridge brings us around a loop which ends at a road now used as a boat launching site. This roadbed marks the location of the original road onto the Great Crossings Bridge.

As the lake's waters recede during times of extreme drought, the roadbed and remnants of the Great Crossings Bridge become visible with the current day Route 40 bridge seen to the south. The concrete foundations of the early 1900s homes that once existed here as the town of Somerville also become visible.

The bronze dedication marker that was once attached to the Great Crossings Bridge was seen during our stop at the Addison Toll House. It was rescued before the valley filled and now stands attached to the large stone next to the toll house.

Great Crossings was significant in the early history of this area as the only section of the Youghiogheny River which could be forded by wagons and travelers on foot. The crossing was regularly used by local Indians, early settlers, and General Braddock's troops on their march to Fort Duquesne.

Remnants of the original Braddock Road approach this area at an angle from the south side of the current day Route 40 before ending at the lake.

FARMINGTON - FORT NECCESITY

Having crossed the Youghiogheny River the road begins to rise as it leads toward our next stop at Farmington, Pennsylvania.

Located here are two sites significant to early American history. The reconstructed Fort Necessity, a National Battlefield Park, and the Mount Washington Tavern, a major stopping point for early travelers along the National Road are both worthy of stopping to take a closer look.

Fort Necessity was a hastily built compound created under the direction of a young George Washington during a retreat from a losing encounter with French and Indian troops at the Great Meadow. On July 3, 1754, it would become the site of a battle that has been characterized by some historians as the start of the French and Indian War. Looking at this small compound, the modern-day visitor becomes quite aware of the poorly defensible location, completely in the open and surrounded by marshy fields.

As a result of this hasty tactical decision, Washington and his men were unable to hold out against the enemy fire. Washington was forced to accept and sign a surrender agreement with the French troops in order to minimize the continued bloodshed and loss of life to the men he commanded.

Unable to read the language the document was written in, Washington would later discover he had not only surrendered, but also declared his involvement in crimes completely unknown to him. Fortunately for our country, Washington in his later years went on to become a much better military strategist and a powerful leader.

Leaving the Fort Necessity National Battlefield Park we will continue west to the top of the ridge behind the fort and stop at the Mount Washington Tavern. Named in honor of George Washington and overlooking the Fort Necessity site, the tavern is believed to have been built around 1828. The large brick building saw a brisk business as the many stagecoach travelers en route to Uniontown, Pennsylvania passed along this section of the National Road. The Mount Washington Tavern was owned and run by the Sampey family until the mid 1800s and was notable for good food and exceptional cleanliness - unusual for this type of facility during the National Road's heyday.

A short distance beyond the Mount Washington Tavern is a small park containing a monument to General Braddock, who was mortally wounded during the battle at Fort Duquesne (near modern day Pittsburgh). During the retreat from Fort Duquesne, General Braddock succumbed to his wounds the evening of July 13, 1755. His body was carried by wagon back to this site where the young George Washington made the decision to bury the body in the middle of the roadbed. After a short memorial service Washington ordered all of the soldiers and wagons should pass over the site, thus disguising the grave. Washington's main fear was that the French and Indian fighters would discover and recognize General Braddock's body and use it for a psychological advantage over the Americans.

It was not until the late 1900s, using modern technology that the actual location of the body was established and the remains removed to the hilltop site for burial beneath the monument.

Alongside the monument a remnant of the original Braddock Road can be seen and a short walk down this trail leads to the marker showing the site where General Braddock was originally buried.

OHIOPYLE & FRANK LLOYD WRIGHT

As we leave the Farmington area behind, our trip continues west until it reaches the area known as Chalk Hill and the historic Stone House Inn.

The old Stone House Inn was another popular stopping point and rest area for travelers along the early National Road and today hosts a restaurant with lodging.

The Stone House Inn - Chalk Hill, PA

As the road continues up the grade past the inn, Chalk Hill Road enters from the right near the crest of the hill. Turning off of the National Road at this spot leads us on an interesting side trip of five or six miles along Chalk Hill Road to Kentuck Knob, the first of two Frank Lloyd Wright designed houses in this area. Continuing past Kentuck Knob bring us to the riverside town of Ohiopyle and a few miles beyond that we arrive at the world-famous Wright creation of Fallingwater. Set in a secluded forest and designed to cantilever out over a nearby stream and cliffs, Fallingwater is the best known of Mr. Wright's many uniquely designed creations. Both houses are worth visiting for a view into the designs used by this master architect.

We will now return south along Chalk Hill Road and upon reaching the National Road we resume our journey to the west.

The entrance to the Frank Lloyd Wright designed home KENTUCK KNOB - Ohiopyle, PA

FALLINGWATER - Probably the best known Frank Lloyd Wright designed home in existence. Near Ohiopyle, PA
Photograph © Cynthia A. Poole

CHESTNUT RIDGE - SUMMIT HOTEL

    The road now begins to travel up the extremely steep grade of Chestnut Ridge. It is interesting to note that when Congress voted to begin the National Road, one key stipulation mandated that no road grade would exceed 5% in severity. It would seem the builders in this section were unable to determine the actual inclination here or more likely, due to local efforts to have the road built here, ignored this part of the mandate. Depending on whether one is traveling on the east or west side, the grade of Chestnut Ridge is 8% to 9%, making it one of the steepest sections encountered across the entire National Road.

    We can only imagine the strain placed on early horse drawn wagons to climb this section of road, and the fear they must surely have encountered when descending the ridge.

    Today's traveler reaches the crest of Chestnut Ridge to find it occupied by the well known Summit Hotel, which offers a commanding view westward toward the towns of Hopwood and Uniontown, Pennsylvania located at the foot of the ridge.

HOPWOOD

Descending the western grade of Chestnut Ridge towards Hopwood will easily provide a severe test of any vehicle's braking system. At the base of the mountain, the original course of the National Road bears right to enter downtown Hopwood.

A short distance after entering into the town we see a historical marker on the right shoulder denoting a side street - Baker Alley - as an important part of the Underground Railroad.

Beyond this point the road splits into east and west bound separate one-way paths of travel as we encountered in downtown Hagerstown, Maryland.

Proceeding through town to the west end of Hopwood, the road leads us into the outskirts of Uniontown providing an excellent view of the city as we are descending towards it.

Upon entering the Uniontown city limits, the traveler must be careful to follow the National Road markers in order to properly navigate through the downtown area. Uniontown is another city with a now divided National Road path through the downtown area.

As we near the center of Uniontown the road passes through a part of the original downtown area and intersects with Route 220. It is here that we will turn left and head south for an interesting side trip to a historic site - Friendship Hill at Point Marion, Pennsylvania - which has a very strong connection to the founding of the National Road.

FRIENDSHIP HILL

Traveling south on Route 220 for approximately 10 to 12 miles bring us to a halfway point, between Uniontown, Pennsylvania and Morgantown, West Virginia, at the small town of Point Marion, Pennsylvania. A right turn onto Route 166 and a three mile drive leads to the entrance lane of the home known as Friendship Hill.

Situated high on a bluff overlooking the Monongahela River, building began here during 1798 and was finished during 1824. The house, located in what was then frontier, became the home of Albert Gallatin and his family. Gallatin would reside here for only a few years before his family's pleas brought them back to the more civilized area of Washington, D.C. Now a National Historic site operated by the National Park Service, the home showcases Albert Gallatin, an early proponent of a national road to the west.

Albert Gallatin supported the creation of a national road to open the west to expansion as early as the late 1700s. Through his friendship with George Washington, Thomas Jefferson, and James Madison he continually promoted the need for a road to enable westward expansion. As the Secretary of the Treasury under President Thomas Jefferson, he continued his support for this undertaking and saw it come to pass when Jefferson signed the bill establishing the National Road.

A Swiss emigrant, Gallatin was well known during his career for his skills in creating a balanced Federal budget, his efforts in the Louisiana Purchase, his scientific endeavors, securing the funding for the Lewis & Clark exploration, and his service to his adopted country.

During the Lewis and Clark expedition, when the two explorers arrived at the then unnamed three forks of the Missouri River, the explorers pronounced the rivers to be the Jefferson, the Madison, and the Gallatin, honoring the two great leaders as well as Gallatin.

Though little known today, Gallatin was well known throughout the world during his lifetime. After serving under President Jefferson he would continue to serve his adopted country under President Madison.

Above - The back of the house at Friendship Hill as seen from the cliff side gazebo.

Below - a view of the Monongahela River looking toward Point Marion, PA from the gazebo at Friendship Hill

Leaving Friendship Hill we will now return to Uniontown from our side trip and upon reaching the National Road we will turn left to continue west.

UNIONTOWN

An original stone National Road mile marker still stands at the side of Main Street as we near the west end of the downtown area. A short distance ahead we will approach the area where the east and west sections of the National Road return to a single bidirectional road and come to Marshall Park.

Marshall Park is a memorial park dedicated to General George C. Marshall by his hometown of Uniontown, Pennsylvania. It displays panels telling of Marshall's life and accomplishments, and contains a large flag display.

On the right side of the street is a parking area and a landscaped park. Within the park is a sculptured likeness of General George C. Marshall sitting on a bench and surrounded by interpretive panels which contain both quotes and a history of the man.

Driving west from Uniontown the road passes the Searight Toll House, the third and last toll house remaining of the original eight that were built along the National Road.

This building, built with red brick, is open to visitors on a somewhat sporadic schedule. The toll house now serves as a museum of life during the early days of the National Road.

BRIAR HILL AND THE PETER COLLEY TAVERN

As we pass the Searight Toll House and continue west we come next to the area known as Briar Hill. Once a major coke ore producing area it is said to have had hundreds of coke furnaces lining the valleys during the early 1900s. To our right is an American icon remaining from the 1950s, an outdoor movie theater or Drive-In.

Passing the Drive-In the road now approaches the deteriorating remains of the Peter Colley Tavern.
Built by Peter Colley in 1796, the building was maintained as a tavern and resting point for stagecoaches and travelers along the road. This is one of the oldest original buildings still standing on the National Road corridor.

Unfortunately, time has not been kind to the Colley Tavern as the building continues to deteriorate despite numerous efforts to save it and the assurance of current owners it would be restored to its historical significance. Each trip past the Colley Tavern over a six year period has revealed little being done to stabilize or protect this important early American site.

While the dense overgrowth of brush has been cleared from the front of the building and some windows covered with acrylic sheeting, there are still many openings into the structure and signs of further deterioration.

Disruption to the area around it through heavy mining equipment and now a planned upscale development along the east end of the property further threaten the future of the building. Just past the tavern stands a very small wooden building, also a victim of years of deterioration. A close inspection shows red and blue paint and a small sign indicating this was once a Post Office. Whether it served the area of Briar Hill or only the mining development behind it is not indicated.

Only the passage of time will tell if the endangered Peter Colley Tavern will continue to survive.

Above - The still standing, but deteriorating, Peter Colley Tavern

Below left - The cornerstone of the Colley Tavern indicates it was built by P&H Colley in 1796

Below right - This small building served as a Post Office for the community that grew up around the coal and coke industry that once flourished in the valley behind it. A single house remains visible in the distance.

BROWNSVILLE

We now arrive at the town of Brownsville, Pennsylvania (founded 1765), a small river-town that still retains much of its early charm.

Standing on a hill top on the eastern end of Brownsville is Nemacolin's Castle. The house was built by local merchant and industrialist Jacob Bowman, who named the site in honor of Chief Nemacolin who had guided settlers to the area.

The home began at the site of Bowman's trading post, thought to have originally been an Indian mound, and during the early to mid 1800s evolved into the rambling twenty two room house seen today. The hilltop location allows one to overlook the Monongahela River and the original downtown area of Brownsville.

A short drive down the grade towards the river valley brings us into the Market Street area as the National Road passes the historic Flatiron Building. Alongside the building the railroad station and tracks still stand. The street continues on past once elegant buildings with carved storefronts and leaves visitors with the impression this was once a prosperous town.

Though the Market Street area has deteriorated, the Brownsville Area Renovation Council is hard at work in their attempts to revitalize this area and restore the town to its former glory. Market Street crosses the Dunlap Creek Bridge, said to be the first cast iron bridge built in the United States. Built during the early 1800s and now hidden by the current road surface, visitors can park in a nearby lot and look underneath to see the intricate original structure.

A right turn in the center of town carries us onto a steel bridge over the Monongahela River and into the west end of Brownsville. Here the road begins a long ascent from the river bottom until reaching the ridge top and rejoining the current day Route 40.

Above - The historic Flatiron Building in downtown Brownsville, PA. The building derives its name from a wedge shaped design, when viewed from above, similar to the shape of an early clothes iron of the same name.

Below - The Dunlap Creek Bridge, said to be the first cast iron bridge built in America.

The Monongahela River bridge carries the National Road across it's namesake river. In the background is the current day Route 40 bridge undergoing maintenance and repair.

At this point the road makes a number of small detours from the current day Route 40 in order to travel along the original route of the National Road through the small towns of Centerville, Richieville, and then Beallsville, Pennsylvania.

Returning to Route 40 we pass the location of the first of five Madonna of the Trail monuments found along the National Road Corridor. A total of twelve statues were placed along the highway on the route of the National Old Trails Road by the Daughters of the American Revolution to honor the early pioneer women who traveled these roads.

Continuing west along Route 40, the road travels deeper into the interior of southwest Pennsylvania until reaching the area known best as Scenery Hill.

Here we will find numerous small shops and the still operating historic Century Inn. Built in 1794 and originally known as Hill's Tavern, the Century Inn continues operation providing food and lodging for an enjoyable experience.

Above - A street scene in the National Road town of Centerville, PA

Below - A mid 1900s gas station now serves duty as storage near Centervile. Note the row of light sockets around the edge of the canopy and the larger central light fixture, both common on this style of building.

Above - The Century Inn at Scenery Hill. In operation since 1794

Below - A canopied building, now a store, appears to have been a 1900s auto repair shop -note the large doors.

WASHINGTON, PA

Traveling on to Washington, Pennsylvania (formed 1781) we see the name of the National Road changes to Chestnut St. or Route 40 and continues with that name until we leave through the west end of town.

Reaching the west end, Route 40 continues past and around a small ridge while a spur of the original National Road can be seen running up the ridge diagonally to our left. This section of the original road can be followed and passes one of the National Road mile markers before reaching the top of the ridge and winding back down the west side where it once again rejoins Route 40.

As we leave Washington and head west, the road passes through a section known as Lincoln Hill before it continues toward the town of Claysville.

Located along the section of road between Lincoln Hill and Claysville, at the intersection with PA Route 221, are the remnants of an early National Road **S** Bridge.

Parking along Route 221 at this site and walking a short distance up the hillside opposite the bridge will allow us to view the **S** form for which the bridge is named. Note the western most end of the bridge's **S** was cut off during the relocation of the road to the current day path of Route 40.

S Bridges were designed with a sharply curving section at each end and a straight span crossing the river or creek below. The curved sections effectively slowed any wheeled traffic and the short, straight section made for the most direct method of spanning a river. An interesting engineering design, the **S** Bridge was intended to cut the building costs of the specialized supports needed to cross a river at an angle. **S** Bridges will be found from here through the state of Ohio, with the best surviving examples of this unique architecture found in Ohio.

CLAYSVILLE

As we continue west we come to the outskirts of the town of Claysville. Nearing the center of Claysville (founded 1812) the road crosses a small modern bridge which covers the framework of an original cut-stone bridge of the keystone design built during the 1800s. Parking nearby, a short walk down the grade allows a view of the underside which shows the remains of the original bridge.

West of Claysville we will turn left, going under the Interstate, from Route 40 in order to stay on the path of the original National Road while the modern Route 40 continues straight ahead. Taking the path of the original road through the countryside gives the feeling early travelers had driving on a narrow rural road with little but scenery to accompany you.

A few miles ahead the road crosses one of the original stone bridges identifiable only by the weathered low stone curb on either side of the roadbed. Take the time to stop at this point and walk down into the field below where the keystone structure of the bridge can be observed.

Looking across the valley from here we are able to view over 200 years of history as we stand on this, the original path of the 1800s National Road. The next road that can be seen running along the bottom of the valley is the current Interstate 70 built during the late 1900s, and on the opposite hillside the road we see is the present day Route 40 built during the early 1900s.

Each of these roads represents what was believed to be the most effective route available during its time and each was later retired from regular use by a faster, smoother and more direct line of travel.

Three phases of transportaton history.
The original National Road (foreground), the early 1900s Route 40 (far hillside) and the late 1900s Interstate Route 70 (note the orange truck) seen at the center of the picture.

The National Road now curves slightly south and away from the track of the existing Interstate highway. Once again we are traveling through an area that could easily have been from an earlier time.

As the road climbs the next grade it comes to an open area and makes a sharp turn toward the right, once again heading west. Aside from a large field, only a small modern house and a single large old tree stand at the tightest point of the curve.

This tree grew alongside the now unseen site of one of the last tollhouses that stood on the National Road in Pennsylvania. This particular toll house saw a variety of uses during the early part of the 1900s until, as a vacant shell, it was finally demolished during the 1980s.

The existence of a toll house at this location is marked today only by the presence of the single tree still standing.

WEST ALEXANDER

The road now continues to the crest of the ridge and then starts downhill to the small town of West Alexander, Pennsylvania. This is the last Pennsylvania town encountered before crossing the state line into West Virginia.

A short distance beyond West Alexander the road rejoins the current Route 40 and after turning left we will continue west into the state of West Virginia.

A ghostly reminder of the National Road. Addison, PA.

MIDDLEBOURNE

Middlebourne was also once a busy National Road town, but like so many other towns it was bypassed by modern roads. It is now little more than a residential area with a church, an 1800s tavern building, and a county maintenance facility at the west end.

Traveling beyond the town limits of Middlebourne we will follow the original National Road route for a few miles until we make a slight right turn onto a short spur road. The spur follows the original route and takes us across an early 1800s **S** Bridge to a small park area. This is the only **S** Bridge open to vehicles along the entire National Road Corridor. There is currently talk of closing this remaining artifact to traffic in the coming year due to the high cost of maintenance and concerns about the ability of the structure to safely carry modern loads.

Leaving the **S** Bridge we will continue west until reaching what appears to be a farm lane. At this point we will turn left as the National Road crosses under the Interstate and then make a quick right to continue westward.

A car crosses the Middlebourne, OH **S** *bridge. This is the only* **S** *bridge still open to vehicle traffic though the state of Ohio is planning to close it off due to concerns over safety.*

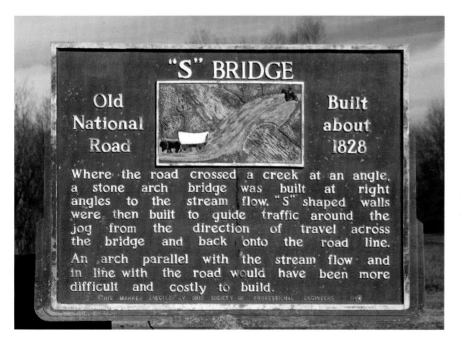

"S" BRIDGE

Old National Road

Built about 1828

Where the road crossed a creek at an angle, a stone arch bridge was built at right angles to the stream flow. "S" shaped walls were then built to guide traffic around the jog from the direction of travel across the bridge and back onto the road line.

An arch parallel with the stream flow and in line with the road would have been more difficult and costly to build.

THIS MARKER ERECTED BY OHIO SOCIETY OF PROFESSIONAL ENGINEERS 1964

The next section of road will carry us to the outskirts of Old Washington, across from a modern day truck stop and restaurant.

Though not the exact original route of the National Road, this section was in use during the early 1900s and gives a traveler a glimpse of travel during earlier times.

An older form of transportation frequently seen on the roads around Middlebourne, OH.

OLD WASHINGTON

Laid out in 1805, the town of Old Washington has the distinction of being the northern most point of battle during the Civil War.

Confederate raiders, having plundered throughout Ohio, came here and were confronted by Union troops. Suffering casualties and the capture of some of their troops, the remaining forces escaped to Northern Ohio but were later captured.

The National Road as it appears through Old Washington, OH.

A short trip west along the National Road from Old Washington brings us to our next stop.

On the left side of the road can be seen a tour marker placed by Guernsey County, Ohio indicating the site of an original section of the brick road bed that carried travelers along the National Road. Now cleared of brush and debris, the road leads downward into a stream valley and gives visitors an idea of the actual size of the road and terrain encountered by the horse drawn wagons and those traveling by foot during the early 1800s.

A glance at a local map indicates an existing current road slightly ahead named Brick Road. This road runs parallel to Route 40 on our left.

Though Brick Road is a paved modern road, driving it will allow us to trace the track followed by the original brick portion of the National Road from the stream crossing up the ridge and back out to the modern day Route 40.

CAMBRIDGE

Next the National Road reaches the outskirts of the city of Cambridge, Ohio.

Cambridge was the birthplace and childhood home of actor William Boyd. Today, William Boyd is best remembered for his portrayal of the popular cowboy hero Hopalong Cassidy on television during the 1940s and early 1950s.

Cambridge is the site of the Hopalong Cassidy Museum and each year the city hosts the annual Hopalong Cassidy Festival which is held during the first weekend of May. The multi-day festival plays host to still living cowboy stars of movie and television fame as well as many re-enactors portraying early cowboy heroes.

Above - A large crowd of cowboy hero look alikes on stage surrounding Grace Bradley Boyd, widow of the late William Boyd, an actor better known as Hopalong Cassidy

Left - Grace Bradley Boyd addresses the auditorium filled with Hopalong Cassidy fans attending the annual Hopalong Cassidy Festival in Cambridge, Ohio.

NEW CONCORD

Following the National Road out of Cambridge and heading toward New Concord the route soon passes a park on the right. At this site we find another preserved **S** Bridge in the area known as Cassell Station.

Further along, the road enters the town of New Concord which was laid out during 1828 in anticipation of the coming section of the National Road.

New Concord is the site of the boyhood home of William Rainey Harper and Robert Francis Harper. William Harper was the founding president of the University of Chicago, while his brother Robert became internationally known as an expert on the ancient people of Assyria.

The Harper House, a log cabin now fully restored, is currently used as a museum.

Located directly across the National Road from the Harper House is the main entrance to Muskingum College, a traditional liberal-arts institute, serving Ohio since 1837.

New Concord is perhaps best known as the boyhood hometown of astronaut and Ohio Senator John Glenn and his wife Annie Glenn, a fact proudly displayed on a sign at each end of the main street.

His boyhood home, moved onto a prominent lot along the National Road near the center of town, is now operated as a museum open to the public.

Leaving the New Concord town limits we reach another area containing a section of the original track of the National Road and the best example of a restored early National Road **S** Bridge still in existence in Ohio.

Visitors can park and take time to walk across the brick paved surface. Steps and a well maintained path lead down to the stream's edge for a better view of the construction and underside of the bridge.

At the east end of the park we find a picnic area and historical markers telling the history of the road and the bridge including early 1900s photographs. Facing the bridge we see Fox Creek Road on the right, a small road with a few houses visible through the trees. It was here that John Glenn's father built the original family home, now relocated, that we passed in town.

Standing on the bridge during late Fall or Winter and looking west we are able to observe a large house overlooking the National Road from the bluff on the right. During most of the year the structure is obscured from view by the large trees that surround it. This hilltop house, due to the efforts of Robert West Speer, played an important role in the Underground Railroad in the 1800s and has been mentioned in a variety of articles describing the significant part the state of Ohio played in the Underground Railroad freedom movement.

THE ZANE GREY & NATIONAL ROAD MUSEUM

A few miles beyond the Fox Creek S Bridge park we arrive at the area known as Norwich, Ohio.

Today the Norwich area seems to be little more than an intersection with the usual gas station, motel and restaurant as a result of the Interstate highway bypassing the area.

Norwich has the major distinction of being home to the Zane Grey & National Road Museum. The museum is dedicated to the preservation of the history of the National Road along with artifacts from the life of famous author Zane Grey who was born and raised nearby.

The nearby city of Zanesville, Ohio was named after the family and throughout eastern Ohio the National Road follows the path of a road originally created by Ebenezer Zane and known as Zane's Trace. Zane's Trace ran from the banks of the Ohio River at Wheeling, West Virginia to Zanesville, Ohio before turning and continuing south. When the National Road was created it followed the path of the earlier road in order to simplify construction efforts.

Here in the museum can be found a replica of Zane Grey's study and a large diorama of life on the National Road during the 1800s construction. The museum also houses numerous artifacts along with a covered wagon and a few cars from the early period of National Road history. Of special interest to many visitors is the extensive display of early Zanesville Pottery, many pieces beautifully and elaborately decorated.

Scattered about the grounds outside the museum are a number of mile markers from various parts of Ohio and a few examples of the early machinery used to construct the state's roads including the National Road.

Above - early automobiles on display at the Zane Grey & National Road Museum

Below - Part of the National Road diorama at the Zane Grey & National Road Museum.

Above & left - A National Road mile marker in front of the City Hall in West Jefferson, OH. When the more modern building was constructed the builders fortunately preserved this piece of American history.

Next the National Road passes through the multiple towns of Alton, West Jefferson, Lafayette, Summerford, Brighton, and Harmony, until finally arriving at the east end of the city of Springfield, Ohio.

Above - The historic Red Brick Tavern, built in 1837, sits along the National Road in Lafayette, Ohio. Looking much like it did during the early days of the road when visited by the common man and by Presidents, it continues to function as a restaurant today.

SPRINGFIELD

From here, tracing the National Road becomes difficult. The path is broken up, but generally follows the main street through downtown Springfield, Ohio. With limited posted signage, we keep moving in the right direction.

Beyond Springfield the route takes us through the small communities of Brandt and Phoneton, both of which are on the outskirts of Dayton, Ohio which is located immediately to the south.

Main Street - Springfield, OH

There are stories told locally of numerous early National Road travelers, mainly immigrants unfamiliar with the area, reaching the Phoneton area and being told this was the end of the National Road. The confused travelers were then misdirected onto a southwest route towards Dayton, Ohio. The road to Dayton was much better maintained than this section of National Road, and further convinced travelers they were correct to head southwest. This appears to have been an attempt by some individuals to ensure Dayton did not share the fate of other towns bypassed and left to decay by the migration west.

Today Dayton, though not located directly on the National Road, is best known as the location of the Wright Brothers original bicycle shop, the nearby Wright-Patterson Air Force Base, and Huffman Prairie Flying Field. It was here, at Huffman Prairie, the Wrights built a hangar and practiced flight while perfecting the operation and control of their early planes. This landmark gave rise to Ohio's reputation of being the birthplace of aviation.

Continuing beyond the outskirts of Dayton the National Road now proceeds west through the towns of Arlington, Bachman, Lewisburg, and Gettysburg, finally ending near the western border of Ohio at the small town of New Paris.

West Main Street - Springfield, OH

A now deserted Clark County Memorial sits unused and deteriorating along the National Road in Springfield, OH

Left - A National Road placard sits outside a local business near Brandt, OH. The road runs along the background at the left of the image.

Because the support post sign had been damaged by trucks making deliveries, a local man created the timber edged flower garden around it to preserve and protect this glimpse into the road's history.

Above - No longer prosperous due to being bypassed by the nearby Interstate Highway, a service station now sits empty and deteriorating in a weed filled lot. East of New Paris, OH.

Below Left - A local curiosity, the water-filled "footprint" depression in a rock at the edge of the service station lot.

Below right - Even the sign advertising the footprint rock shows signs of neglect and age.

Though located a short distance north of the National Road, New Paris (1817) became prominent in the manufacturing and supply of lime and stone from local quarries. This was possible due to the number of large limestone deposits found in the area. The town is also known as the home of Reverend Benjamin Hanby, the author of an early Christmas Carol titled "Up On The House Top" which he wrote in 1864.

Leaving New Paris, we will travel the National Road for about a mile until it crosses the Ohio - Indiana border and enters the state of Indiana at the city of Richmond.

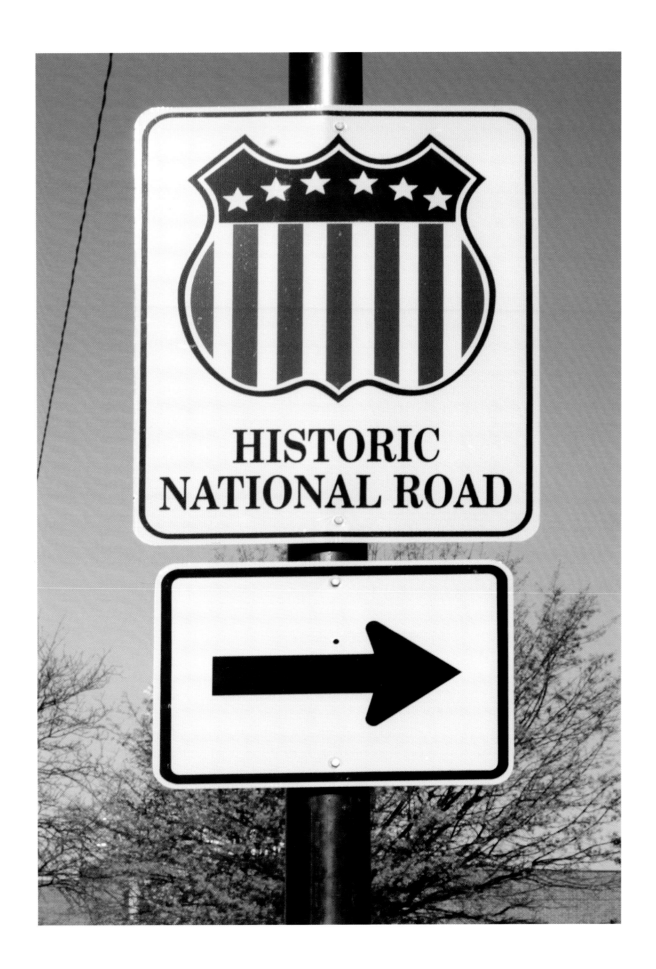

INDIANA

RICHMOND

Entering Indiana at the outskirts of Richmond, the National Road appears as a straight line extending into the city and on toward the western horizon. By some accounts, the original survey work for the coming National Road was completed into the Richmond area about 1827.

A short distance toward town, after passing under a railroad bridge is the National Road Visitor's Center located on the left side of the road. The Wayne County, Indiana Tourism office is well worth visiting for the excellent brochures and information available on the many historic sites and points of interest found in Richmond.

Richmond, Indiana has also been known as Rose City due to the large commercial floral gardens started in the late 1800s and for the state of the art rose research and hybridization efforts which continue today.

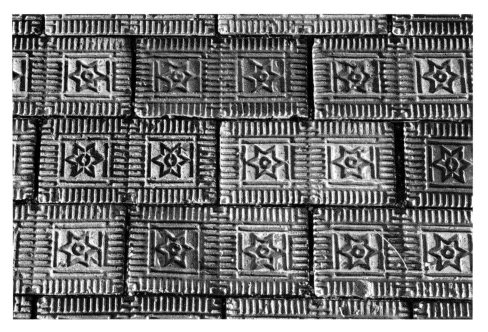

Traveling closer to downtown Richmond, Indiana we pass the Starr Historic District - a large area of restored historic homes, the expansive Glen Miller Park, an All American Rose garden, the Wayne County Historical Society overflowing with artifacts of early life, and finally reach the downtown historic district with its brick inlaid sidewalks.

While walking in the downtown historic district, notice that most of the glazed paving bricks on the sidewalks have a star shaped pattern embedded into them, a tribute to Richmond's past.

At the west end of town stands the Wayne County Courthouse. Built from local stone and surrounded by extensive garden, the Courthouse dominates the landscape.

Passing the courthouse the National Road crosses the Whitewater River Gorge. The wide plain carved by the river was the original location of the Starr Piano Co. and Gennett Records. Known as the Cradle of Recorded Jazz, Gennett Records was one of the earliest recording studios and instrumental to the growth of Jazz. Many famous jazz musicians recorded here, among them Bing Crosby, Hoagy Carmichael, Louis Armstrong, Bix Beiderbecke, Jelly Roll Morton, and Tommy Dorsey. The city of Richmond is sometimes referred to as Starr City due to the Starr Piano Co. prominence in building pianos which were often featured in early recorded music.

Another point of interest is the trail through the Whitewater River Gorge. Walking here we can see numerous piles of stone rubble containing small fossils, many from the Paleozoic era. Broken loose from the sidewalls of the gorge by the actions of time and water, the stones reveal their secrets. Removal of fossils is discouraged, but the fossil sites are easily viewed along the path, especially the southern end of the trail.

Continuing west past the Whitewater River Gorge to the outskirts of Richmond the National Road passes Earlham College. The college, founded by the Society of Friends during 1847, teaches Liberal Arts & Science surrounded by a tranquil park-like landscaping conducive to quiet reflection.

The All American Rose Garden located at the east end of Richmond, IN. In the background a wedding party prepares for the ceremony at the gazebo on the gardens grounds.

Above - A mural painted on the side of a Richmond, IN building honors the heritage of Gennett Records and the Starr Piano Company of Richmond. The mural was painted by local artist Pam Bliss Ferguson.

Below - The Wayne County Courthouse located along the National Road in Richmond, IN.

Above left - The graceful arches of the now demolished bridge that carried the National Road across the Whitewater River Gorge. It has now been replaced by a more modern style of bridge.

Above right - an example of the fossils easily seen at the surface of the hillsides along the Whitewater River Gorge.

Below - The deteriorating remains of the Starr Piano Company factory still stand in the Whitewater River Gorge at Richmond, IN.

Above left - Another of the Richmond murals celebrates the performers who recorded at Gennett Records.

Above right - A sign from the Gennett Record company and an old record player at the Wayne County Museum.

Below - A large section of the Wayne County Museum is dedicated to the history of Richmond's Starr Piano Company, Gennett Records, and the many famous performers who recorded here.

Centerville, Indiana, as the Wayne County Seat, is a small town that grew substantially with the National Road passing through it.

Entering Centerville from the east the traveler can see a restored two story log cabin set back from the north side of the road. This building was the original Wayne County Courthouse until 1873. By that time the population of Richmond had grown to the point of requiring the Courthouse site to be moved to the current larger facility in the city.

Close by to the town of Centerville are the only two National Road mile markers known to exist in Indiana. The first mile marker is located just east of the town at the edge of a residential lawn while the second marker sits in front of an early brick home on the western outskirts of the town.

Leaving Centerville, the road continues west through Pennville, then East Germantown until it reaches the east end of Cambridge City, Indiana.

Left - The first of only two National Road mile markers found in Indiana

Below - The original Wayne County Courthouse at Centerville. It was replaced by the larger stone courthouse at the west end of Richmond.

Above - Main Street of Centerville, IN.

Below left - The historic Lantz House in Centerville now serves as a Bed & Breakfast.

Below right - The second of only two mile markers found in Indiana sits in front of this house at the west end of Centerville.

CAMBRIDGE CITY

Cambridge City, a moderately sized town, greatly benefited through the years by the National Road serving as the main thoroughfare through the town.

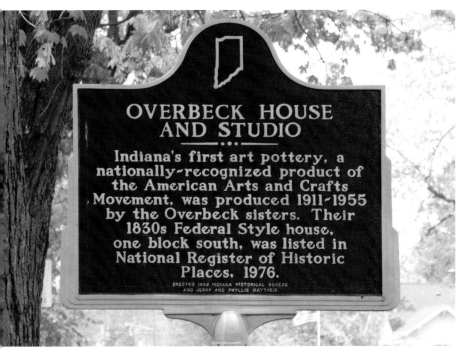

At the east end of town stands a plaque directing visitors to the Overbeck House. This was the site of the Overbeck Pottery, an important style of early American pottery, created in 1911. The six Overbeck sisters, though not all involved in physically creating the pottery, all collectively contributed to the establishment of this pottery art form. The most unique aspect of their work was the insistence on creating the pottery from ideas and designs they took from nature and their surrounding area. Examples of their influential work can be found throughout the world today.

Located a block north of the National Road is an old gas station, restored to an accurate representation of a 1950s era Texaco station, complete with period displays and signs.

In the same block is a community park and gazebo where you can sit and view the unique architecture on the surrounding buildings. Pay close attention to the copper weather vane atop the gazebo - the covered wagon and team pay homage to the early years of the city and the National Road.

Each year Cambridge City conducts a large festival celebrating Canal days as recognition of the nearly forgotten canals built throughout the state that served as another means of transportation and commerce.

The historic Vinton House - Cambridge City, IN

Above - A plaque describing the East Germantown Civil War Band's part in the conflict.

Right - A window in an East Germantown storefront prominently displays a sign telling travelers they are on U.S. Route 40 - The National Road.

Left - A 1910 Empire Auto parked in front of the vintage gasoline pumps at the restored mid 1900s Texaco station in Cambridge City, IN.

The car was one of the many vehicles participating in the 2001 Antique Auto Tour of the National Road.

MT. AUBURN - HUDDLESTON FARMHOUSE

Passing the western outskirts of Cambridge City, the road arrives at the area known as Mount Auburn, Indiana.

On the left side of the road we see a large white building and an adjacent barn. This is the Huddleston Farmhouse Museum, an important Indiana historic site and one of the early stopping places for travelers during the heyday of the National Road.

The museum has been restored by, and is operated, by the Historic Landmarks Foundation of Indiana, based in Indianapolis. The lower floor is open to the public for viewing while the upper level currently serves as office space for the Indiana National Road Association.

Numerous original furniture pieces and everyday fixtures remain, allowing visitors to see how an early 1800s family lived.

The original inhabitants seem to have enjoyed a higher standard of living than many living along the early National Road. Despite their level of comfort, a visitor can easily see that when compared to the standards of today life in the early 1800s was still frequently difficult.

Above - A stillroom and sink area located off of the main kitchen space at the Huddleston Farmhouse.

Left - After a meeting of the Indiana National Road Association, members enjoy a dinner prepared on the back lawn of the Huddleston Farmhouse using the cooking methods of the early National Road travelers.

Traveling on, the National Road soon passes through the towns of Dublin, Straughn, Lewisville, and Ogden, Indiana.

DUBLIN

LEWISVILLE

DUNREITH - OLD NATIONAL ROAD SECTION

Traveling west of Ogden we come to the village area of Dunreith, Indiana. Here we will take a detour, turning left from the present day Route 40 in order travel a short section of the original National Road. The trip will take us through countryside that appears little changed from the late 1800s - early 1900s. This section of the original road course continues for approximately three to four miles paralleling the current day Route 40 until it rejoins the newer road just outside of Knightstown, Indiana.

Above - Automobiles participating in the 2001 Antique Auto Tour travel a section of the original National Road between Dunreith and Greenfield, IN.

Right - A show of civic pride in the heritage of the National Road. The Dunreith VFD has painted a map of the road across Indiana and a reproduction of the shield used on the marker signs across the state.

Photo © Donna J. Tauber.

KNIGHTSTOWN

Upon returning to Route 40, we turn left to continue our journey into Knightstown, Indiana.

The Hoosier Gym, a local high school gymnasium was the location for the filming of the 1985 movie ***Hoosiers*** starring Gene Hackman. Now restored and serving as a community center, the gym is open to the public for tours.

This section of the National Road is a part of Indiana's famous Antique Alley and home to numerous unique shops.

We will now leave Knightstown and travel on through Charlottesville and Cleveland before reaching our next stop at Greenfield, Indiana.

GREENFIELD - CUMBERLAND

Entering Greenfield, Indiana the visitor first notices the striking appearance of the massive Hancock County Courthouse at the east end of town.

This is another example of the ornate stone courthouse found in abundance across the National Road.

Greenfield, Indiana is perhaps best known as the birthplace of beloved Hoosier Poet James Whitcomb Riley. His restored home, the Riley House, is located west of the town square along the National Road. The building, open to the public, also serves as a museum of Hancock County history.

As we continue our journey west along the National Road we pass Riley Park, named in honor of poet James Whitcomb Riley.

Near the entrance to the park stands the old 1853 two story log jailhouse which was originally located nearer to the town square. Today the log structure serves as a museum of early pioneer life in Indiana and is open to the public.

Above - The birthplace of Hoosier Poet James Whitcomb Riley. Greenfield, IN

Below - The restored log jail house, now a museum, in Riley Park. Greenfield, IN.

As we leave Greenfield the road travels through the towns of Philadelphia and Gem before entering Cumberland Indiana.

Cumberland, Indiana (1831) was named after the city of Cumberland, Maryland - the eastern terminus of the National Road. The city prospered from the large volume of traffic as it was an important stopping point for west bound travelers along the National Road. Cumberland, once a relatively large and independent city on its own, has now become a suburb to pass through on the trip to downtown Indianapolis, Indiana.

INDIANAPOLIS

A limousine company with a sense of humor. On the National Road (Washington Street) in east Indianapolis, IN

As we enter the eastern end of Indianapolis (1821), the capital of Indiana, the National Road becomes known as Washington Street. This name will be seen until the road exits the west side of the city en route to Plainfield, Indiana. It should be noted, although the National Road was beneficial to the growth and development of Indianapolis, the remainder of the National Road across the state of Indiana was not completed until the 1830s.

The east end of Washington Street appears as an older, industrialized section of the city, but with a number of small parks and a revived interest in the many historic community areas. The Irvington Historic District (1870) located on the east side of town and immediately south of the National Road is an excellent example of the efforts being put forth at revitalization.

Entering the downtown area we pass the Indiana Repertory Company housed in the 1927 Indiana Theater building with its impressive carved façade. It is worth taking the time to stop and admire the features of this unique building. When open, the carvings and fixtures can be seen inside the building and are even more ornate. Located on the second floor hall the theater houses a number of lavish costumes and artifacts from earlier productions.

Located a block north of the intersection of Meridian and Washington Street at the center of the city, is the 284 foot tall Soldiers' and Sailors' Monument, constructed in 1901. The circular area occupied today by the monument was the original site of the Governor's Mansion. It was known formerly as Governor's Circle until the mansion was demolished and relocated in 1857. The monument is 342 feet in diameter at the base and contains the Colonel Eli Lilly Civil War Museum housed at street level. An observation area at the top of the monument is open to the public and offers a panoramic view of downtown Indianapolis.

The Indiana Repertory Theater - building on left.

The Central Canal, running north to south through the center of the city, began in 1836 with a plan to create a two hundred and ninety six mile long waterway for the transportation of commerce. Because the State of Indiana became bankrupt from defaults on the large number of loans initiated to finance the project, only a short section slightly over eight miles in length was ever completed. Today the Central Canal enjoys a rebirth of use as a popular tourist attraction and a pedestrian connector to various parts of the city.

On the west side of town we pass the White River State Park, the Indianapolis Zoo, the White River Gardens with a large enclosed butterfly house, the Indiana State Museum, and a number of other impressive public facilities. The White River State Park holds the distinction of being the only state park in Indiana located completely within the boundaries of a city.

Located close by in this area are numerous points of interest including the Eiteljorg Museum of American Indians and Western Art and the NCAA Hall of Champions.

Travelers venturing toward the north end of town may enjoy the historic Walker Theatre, and the Arts District. Of course, any discussion of Indianapolis would be incomplete if we failed to mention the legendary Indianapolis Motor Speedway, home of the Indianapolis 500, located a short ride north of the downtown area.

Left - The home where James Whitcomb Riley lived as an adult. Now preserved as a museum, it is located in the Lockerbie Square section of east Indianapolis.

Right - Master coppersmith Michael Bonne stands with some of his work and in front of an article describing his former shop located on the National Road.

Originally located in Knightstown, Michael now operates a shop near the National Road at the east end of Indianapolis, IN.

Students and other guests assist IN First Lady Judy O'Bannon (center), in the ribbon cutting ceremony held on May 8th, 2003. The ceremony was held at the same time in each of the six states making up the National Road corridor to celebrate the US Department of Transportation designating the National Road as an All American Road.
Photo © Wayne Goodman, Historic Landmarks Foundation of Indiana.

Right - A couple enploys a pedal car to enjoy a liesurely tour of the downtown section of Indianapolis

Left - The Soldiers and Sailors Monument located on the circle as seen from Meridian Street and Washington Street. There is an observation deck at the top of the tower where visitors can get a view of the downtown area.

In the base of the monument is the Lilly Civil War Museum. The entrance can be seen in this photo.

Right - A marker memorializing the National Road sits along the National Road (Washington Street) in front of the Indiana State House.

It was given to the state by the Daughters of the American Revolution during a ceremony held at the site in 1916,

Left - Interesting Indian designs and the detailed carved heads cover the entrance of the Old Trail Building on the road in downtown Indianapolis, IN

Right - Spring time comes to Veterans Memorial Park located behind the Soldiers and Sailors Monument near the National Road.

Above and right - Two views of the Central Canal which runs through the heart of Indianapolis.

Below left - The historic Walker Theater near downown Indianapolis

Below right - An interpretive placard on a corner opposite the Walker Theater tells the story of a vibrant 1890s district well known for it's theaters, jazz clubs, and social atmosphere.

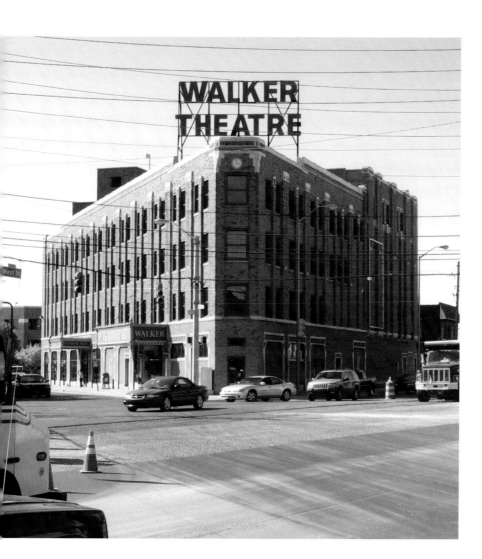

Above - An elaborate wildlife sculpture graces the lawn in front of the Eiteljorg Museum of American Indians and Western Art. The sculpture is easily seen from the National Road.

Below - The Conservatory / Butterfly House of White River Gardens. Bordered by the National Road to the south and the White River on the east, White River State Park is the only Indiana State Park located completely within city limits.

Left - One of the many entrances to the Indianapolis Motor Speedway

Right - A group of Motorcycle Police Officers leads the 2002 Indiana Antique Auto Tour group across the legendary "Yard of Bricks" on a lap around the Indianapolis Motor Speedway.

The officers graciously volunteered their time to this event.

Left - Participants in the 2002 Antique Auto Tour of the National Road line up their vehicles in anticipation of a lap around the Indianapolis Motor Speedway.

Above - The grave of beloved Hoosier Poet, James Whitcomb Riley, overlooks a commanding view of the downtown Indianapolis skyline to the south.

Below - The Indianapolis skyline at night. As viewed from the west side of the city at the edge of the White River.

PLAINFIELD

A still operating remnant of another era, a roadside diner at Plainfield, IN.

We now leave Indianapolis and travel into Plainfield, Indiana. Plainfield is the site of the Friends Church facility known as the Western Yearly Meeting House. During the 2002 Indiana Antique Auto Tour the meeting house served as a Tour stop.

The National Road continues west through Belleville (1829), then on to Stilesville (1828) now primarily a residential town with numerous houses remaining from the late 1800s, and continues through Mount Meridian as we travel next to Putnamville, Indiana.

The roadside motel, a disappearing icon of the early days of National Road travel.

PUTNAMVILLE

Entering Putnamville (1830) the road continues on past the Indiana State Prison on the left and a unique Art Deco style State Police Barracks located on the right.

NOTE : In this area traffic along the road is prohibited from stopping due to the nearby location of a prison facility.

Above - The Art Deco styled State Police Barrakcs at Putnamville, IN.

Below - Three centuries of National Road transportation - An 1800s horse drawn covered wagon (foreground), a 1910 Empire automobile (back), and the 2001 Rose Hulman Solar Phantom automobile (middle) powered by the sun.

Above - Reminiscent of a scene from the early 1900s, a group of antique automobiles cross a bridge over Deer Creek on a concrete section of the original National Road route near of Putnamville, IN.

Left - Legendary Indianapolis Motor Speedway announcer Tom Carnegie autographing Historic National Road signs. Known as The Voice of the Indianapolis 500, Mr. Carnegie took the time to speak with his many admirers while the 2001 Indiana Antique Auto Tour was stopped for lunch. He also served as the Grand Marshall for the tour. Putnamville, IN.

A few small, unincorporated communities are passed before the National Road reaches Knightsville (established 1844), an area on the outskirts of Brazil, Indiana.

Above - A modern day automobile cruises past a long line of antique car enthusiasts out for a pleasant days ride. This scene is east of Brazil, IN.

Bottom left - A roadside marker tells the story of the 10 o'clock line and the expansion of Indiana through the purchase of lands from numerous Indian tribes.

Bottom right - The McKinley House. Now a Bed and Breakfast situated along the National Road near Brazil, IN, the home was originally built in 1872 by Green McKinley who was a contractor on the National Road during it's construction.

BRAZIL

Reaching Brazil, Indiana the most prominent structure to be seen is again a large courthouse built from local stone. As noted before, at numerous locations across the National Road Corridor, this type of building can generally be expected to be of an impressive size and relatively ornate in design and execution.

The courthouse in Brazil does not disappoint our expectations. Walking inside visitor will find marble accents and a staircase winding towards the dome.

Looking up, an impressively designed stained glass panel at the dome of the building is highlighted.

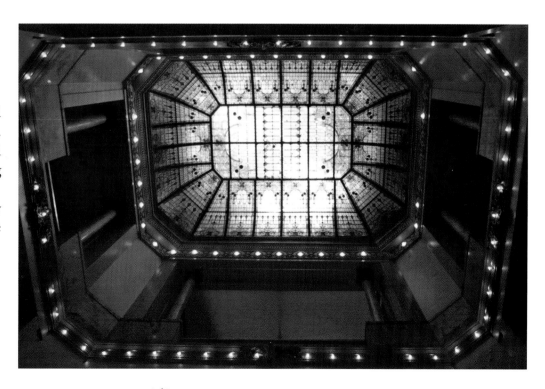

The well-landscaped lawn surrounding the courthouse contains a jet aircraft mounted on a pedestal as a memorial to the many veterans of foreign wars. The tree shaded lawn provided a pleasant backdrop and resting place for participants of the 2002 Indiana Antique Auto Tour.

Leaving Brazil we will continue our drive west through the communities of Seelyville and East Glenn until we reach the city of Terre Haute, Indiana.

Classical Revival style Post Office building, now the Clay County Historical Society Museum. Brazil, IN

Above - Main Street of Greenup, IL with it's patriotically decorated upper story porches

Below - Two older Greenup buildings have been renovated and relocated to the west end of Main Street for use.

Above - Looking toward Greenup from the covered bridge reveals a dark autumn storm front moving toward the town from the east.

Below - A young man enjoys the warm weather to spend time fishing in the Embarras River next to the National Road and the Greenup covered bridge.

The original route of the National Road travels across the recreated Greenup, IL covered bridge.

JEWETT

Main Street - Jewett, Illinois

Returning to the current-day Route 40 a short distance beyond the Greenup covered bridge, we turn right to continue our journey. The current road passes the town of Jewett and the community of Montrose which are situated on a section of the original road running parallel to the modern highway.

Jewett is typical of the small towns that once populated the National Road, only to be left behind as faster, more modern highways were created. With a few small local businesses and signs of more prosperous times, Jewett is now reduced to a pleasant residential town.

MONTROSE

The steeple of a large Catholic Church dominates the skyline of Montrose, Illinois as the National Road enters from the east.

A sign of earlier prosperity, today Montrose has become a residential area with only a few stores and businesses remaining in town while the outlying land is dominated by farms and the ever present railroad tracks.

Main Street - Montrose, Illinois

TEUTOPOLIS

Leaving Montrose we travel to the suburban area of Teutopolis, Illinois. Teutopolis (1830s) manages to retain a great deal of small town charm and character. Despite the proximity of the larger city of Effingham to the west a number of small stores still survive and the town appears to be maintained with a great deal of pride and independence. Of all the small towns we have passed through since entering Illinois, Teutopolis has the feeling of being the most commercially viable.

EFFINGHAM

A few miles west of Teutopolis the National Road leads us into the city of Effingham, Illinois.

Effingham (1853) continues to grow and prosper due to the close proximity of Interstate Route 70 and the high volume of tourism and commercial traffic it carries.

A portion of the original downtown commercial district still remains intact within the vicinity of the courthouse. The surrounding area is mostly residential with well kept and neatly landscaped homes.

Downtown Effingham, Illinois

Once a manufacturing center, the majority of business in Effingham now appears to be connected to commercial shopping areas scattered around the town and the numerous businesses making their home within sight of the interstate highway to the north.

Leaving Effingham, the National Road passes through Ewington, where little remains of the original town, and on to Funkhauser. Funkhauser shows little of a historic past, though a small population and numerous houses still remain.

Effingham Courthouse - built during the late 1800s

The town of Altamont, Illinois appears ahead of us a short distance to the west.

Altamont remains an example of a small Illinois town that continues to thrive as evidenced by the commercial district with numerous stores and the necessary supermarket and bank. It is noteworthy that most of the town of Altamont lies away from the National Road rather than incorporating the road as a main street. This seems to indicate that the railroads, making headway into the area north of town as the National Road was being built, and the much later Interstate corridor further north, were more influential on the current day layout of the town.

ST. ELMO - BROWNSTOWN

Beyond Altamont, the National Road continues west to the town of St. Elmo then on towards Brownstown, Illinois.
Today, both exist as small towns and aside from a few local businesses are mainly residential.

Here again, as in Altamont, we can see the effect of the railroads on the creation of the towns as the main portion of both towns is centered north of the National Road's path.

Little traffic appears on the road into St. Elmo

Left - A roadside motel, now showing signs of deterioration from the loss of business traffic, sits along the road near St. Elmo.

Above - The local equipment company building, though still in good condition, appears to be unoccupied and the equipment lot at the side of the building is nearly empty.

Below - The recent sign at the west end park entrance declaring this to be Gretchen Wilson Park in honor of the singer who has made her hometown proud.

HIGHLAND

Approaching the eastern outskirts of Highland, Illinois, we pass a small brick house decorated with numerous symbols painted on the bricks. The decorations are said to be of German and Swiss origin and are indicative of the nationality of the original settlers of the area.

Entering the town we pass the hospital and continue into the downtown Highland area with more evidence of the town's German and Swiss heritage seen in decorative touches.

Immediately to our right is a small park with a gazebo band shell, a fountain, and in front of the fountain a large three panel mural. Created in the early 1980s by the people of Highland, the mural is a mosaic made up of many different colored tile pieces. The three panels depict historic events that took place here and a map of the downtown area on the center panel.

Located behind the park area, less than a block from the main square, is a section of old buildings that appear to have been built during the early 1900s. Some of the structures now house offices and small businesses. It is a tribute to the foresight of Highland that these buildings have been preserved and are still in use.

From the park the National Road proceeds through the downtown area and bears off to the left at the western end, continuing along again as a two-lane country road.

ST. JACOB and TROY

Beyond Highland we come to the small village of St. Jacob, Illinois (1849), another of the many towns bypassed by the creation of the current day Route 40 and left as little more than a residential cluster of houses.

From St. Jacob we proceed until we reach the town of Troy, Illinois. In order to continue our drive over the original route of the National Road we will only skirt along the outer edge of town.

The National Road was originally the main street through Troy, but with the development of the Interstate Highway System most of the newer construction lies to the north of the original road.

Subsequently, the bulk of the town now lies a distance north of the original path of the National Road similar to what we have seen in a number of other small communities in eastern Illinois.

COLLINSVILLE

Next our journey leads us toward the city of Collinsville, Illinois, the last large town we will encounter before reaching East St. Louis and the vicinity of the Mississippi River.

The National Road as it travels through this area is reminiscent of the mid 1900s, a narrow road with two lanes, no markings, and a raised center crown. In many places particularly near the outskirts of Collinsville, there is little more than wooden posts, some stock fencing, and a narrow grass median separating the National Road from the high speed traffic speeding by on the Interstate.

An example of the little distance between the high speed world and a slower way of life. East of Collinsville, IL.

As we reach Collinsville (1837) the old road ends abruptly at a traffic light and we must turn left onto the more modern four-lane road in order to enter the town.

The historic downtown section of Collinsville remains intact and well preserved though the National Road's east and west routes are separated here by a block as we have seen in other cities across the corridor.

A return trip from the west end of Collinsville to the downtown area can be very confusing for the traveler unfamiliar with the area.

Once again the excellent Historic National Road signs provided by Illinois make the task easier though it is still important to pay close attention to the signs in order to maintain the correct traffic lane as numerous turns throughout the town complicate travel.

One of the most unusual distinctions held by Collinsville is neither very old nor National Road related, but nonetheless interesting. Collinsville is well known as the home of the world's largest catsup bottle.

A one hundred and seventy foot tall water tower in the shape of, and painted to resemble, a giant bottle of Brooks brand catsup stands near the top of a hill on Route 159.

Located a short distance from the National Road and downtown Collinsville, the tower overlooks the former Brooks Food factory where the catsup was originally produced.

During the 1960s the catsup production moved out of state and the factory was later sold. Scheduled for demolition the tower has been preserved due to the efforts of local groups and the publicity they generated. The tower now enjoys a degree of status as a listing on the National Register of Historic Places. It is worth the short side trip to view this unique piece of Americana.

Returning from our side trip, we will continue west until we exit Collinsville along the National Road, known better as Collinsville Road from here to East St. Louis.

After descending a steep grade away from the city, the road turns to a four lane highway as it levels off and we enter the valley created long ago by a young Mississippi River.

As we continue along this section of the National Road we pass older homes, remnants of the building boom of the 1950s and 1960s, and small commercial lots.

A plain looking building formerly housing a gas station or other small business is now hand painted in gaudy colors and patterns reminiscent of the 1960s. Hand painted signs along the shoulder of the road and on the building's façade announce the opening of a tattoo parlor. On a subsequent trip through the area in early 2005, the building was seen to be once again painted solid white and the business was gone, symbolic of the economic stress the area endures.

Most of the homes in this area appear well maintained but many are now beginning to show their age. Some of the numerous business buildings appear neglected in appearance, others look to be vacant or badly deteriorating.

The buildings showing the highest degree of maintenance along this stretch of the road are the few gas stations and the buildings of the Fairmount Park Race Track. The racetrack stands out in stark comparison to the surrounding area because of the well maintained building and the many newer cars, most sporting Missouri license plates, seen in the parking lot whenever the track is open.

The nearby access to the Interstate, seemingly created solely to provide access to the racetrack, shortens the trip and eases the drive from the neighboring state.

A look up and down the National Road in this area gives the traveler an immediate impression that the revenue coming here creates little in the way of a ripple effect to benefit the communities in the surrounding area.

CAHOKIA MOUNDS

As we continue our drive west, in minutes we reach the area of the Cahokia Mounds. It was here that ancient tribes of Indians lived and built a city (approx. 900 A.D.) of up to twenty thousand residents, with numerous earthen mounds for ceremony and burial purposes. The largest of the mounds, Monk's Mound, has been preserved and along with interpretive panels shows the expansive scope of the Indian village.

Monk's Mound is the largest prehistoric earthen mound found in North America. Though the original Indian name for the mound has been lost to time the name Monk's Mound was given later in reference to a group of Trappist Monk's who lived in the area during the 1800s.

Over one hundred feet in height and covering nearly fourteen acres, Monk's Mound was a multi-tiered site and believed to be the center of government for the Indians living here.

The top of Monk's Mound is flat and originally held a large building believed to have been either the Chief's home or the location of tribal government. From the height and open view provided by Monk's Mound, a visitor can look to the southwest and see the nearby Fairmount City area and beyond that the St. Louis, Missouri skyline and the St. Louis Arch.

The mound was originally encircled by a stockade wood-post wall, over two miles in length, with towers located at regular intervals. It is still to be discovered whether the wall was for defense only or served to separate the governing class from the general population.

Modern day archeological excavation is being done in an attempt to determine the original site of the wall and watchtowers. A small portion of the wall showing the overall size and the unique entry passage design has been reconstructed along the northern edge of the site between Monk's Mound and the parking area. Nearby is an ongoing archeological excavation which the visitor can watch.

Though there are steps on the National Road side of the mound that lead to the top level, visitors should be aware there is no parking available along the National Road in front of Monk's Mound. The walk from the designated parking area is over a half a mile in length. Keep in mind the steps are steep and numerous and may present a challenge to those with health problems or disabilities as well as small children.

NOTE : Handicapped parking is available at the lot, but the length of the walk coupled with the steep climb up the many steps makes this site user unfriendly for those with disabilities or for small children who might tire from the walk.

Above - A reconstructed section of the original perimeter fence that surrounded Monk's Mound during the time the Indian civilization lived at this site.

Below - An archaeological excavation at the northeast corner of the fence perimeter. Monk's Mound is seen in the background.

Left - An archaeological excavation pit near Monk's Mound at the Cahokia Mounds site.

The pit is being carefully opened in progressive steps as can be seen by the various levels of soil in front of the worker digging, while details are recorded by the person sitting at the top.

The grid lines of string, necessary to control the digging process, can be seen running from the foreground. At the middle of the pit an uncovered section of one of the original stockade posts can be seen.

Right - The entrance area of the Cahokia Mounds visitors site near East St. Louis, IL.

The painted lines seen in the foreground area are representations of where parts of the ancient village were excavated prior to the building construction.

Inside the Visitors Center we will find large dioramas depicting the daily life events of the original inhabitants of the Cahokia area as well as numerous interpretive displays and artifacts that have been found in the area.

Directly across the National Road from Monk's Mound are numerous smaller mounds and the Cahokia Mounds Visitors Center. It is well worth taking the time for a side trip here in order to see the Center's large collection of artifacts and the reconstructed scenes of early Cahokia village life.

Another unique feature of early civilization found in this area is a circular array of posts now referred to as Woodhenge. The grouping is named for the likeness to the design of Stonehenge in England and is thought to have served a similar purpose for observing sun movement and possible religious ceremony. Woodhenge is located next to the National Road a short distance west of Monk's Mound with abundant parking available.

Little is yet known about the tribes that existed here during the Mississippian Culture era though research is ongoing along with archaeological excavation. It is believed that the early cultures settled in this fertile region due to major rivers joining together a short distance away. Today the entire area is recognized as one of the richest archeological sites in the United States. Efforts continue to race the clock and the developer's bulldozer in an attempt to uncover the secrets of this ancient culture.

Less than fifteen percent of the mounds noted in the Cahokia area during the mid 1800s remain today and many researchers believe Cahokia once extended to the Mississippi River and beyond to the Missouri side. Indeed, evidence uncovered during an excavation at East St. Louis in the early 1990s would tend to confirm this theory.

This area is so important to the study of ancient culture that the United Nations designated the Cahokia Mounds as a World Heritage Site in 1982.

An interesting side note is that the nearby city of St. Louis, Missouri was originally called Mound City by early settlers due to the large number of Indian mounds they saw here. Sadly, during a period of heavy settlement and growth in the early 1800s the mounds were demolished and used as fill to create a more level landscape and the current city was built upon their remains.

FAIRMOUNT CITY - EAST ST. LOUIS

As we travel closer to the end of our trip across the National Road we enter the area known as Fairmount City, Illinois. The area is an older residential suburb local to the city of St. Louis and one of the last Illinois towns before reaching the Mississippi River.

Here the results of the National Road being bypassed by the Interstate routes are, unfortunately, more pronounced. Roadside motels, busy during the prosperous period of the road now stand nearly empty and showing signs of deterioration and minimal upkeep. Nearby the weed choked remains of the Surrey Restaurant sign is barely visible. The restaurant itself, in deteriorating condition for years, was razed during 2004 while a neighboring building continues to decay.

Passing the Surrey Restaurant sign we encounter open two-lane road with little traffic. Houses in the residential sections are interspersed with a few house trailers and all appear well maintained for the most part but, due to age, give the appearance of a forgotten and moribund community.

A short drive beyond the restaurant will bring us to a large flooded section of wetland on the right side of the road. Looking beyond this marshy area we can see the St. Louis Arch beckoning on the skyline. The irony of the disparity between this once prosperous area of the National Road and the bright lights of the big city is the result of the modern Interstate highway, a mere few miles away, completely bypassing and forgetting this area.

The importance of regular travelers through this section, and the results of their disappearance, can be seen in the slowly dying businesses still remaining.

A large wetlands area along the National Road at Fairmount City, IL. The St. Louis, MO skyline is in the background.

Entering the last stretch of road and the upcoming end to our journey we now proceed toward the outskirts of East St. Louis, Illinois.

Approaching an intersection and a four way stop sign we see a lone building on the right. Deteriorating, and now long abandoned, we have arrived at the former Hillcrest Motel.

The ornate trim and the substantial construction of the building speak of an earlier day when this crossroad was busier and the area more prosperous. Today the crossing is easily navigated with no other vehicles in sight.

A short drive past the Hillcrest Motel finds us at the intersection with Route 64. On our right is a deserted gas station covered with the large porcelain coated metal tiles as was common practice during the 1950s and 1960s. To the left is another deserted building, probably a restaurant or diner, situated in the median of this once busy area.

After crossing Route 64 and then a section of railroad track we enter East St. Louis. Here the course of the National Road meanders along making it quite easy to become disoriented and lose the path of the road. Follow the Illinois Historic National Road signs very carefully through this section.

Much neglected, this area suffers from a great deal of urban blight and deteriorating buildings. The road passes by once stately old homes and churches with roof structure and walls collapsing, junked cars along the street, and a generally poor road surface. That hard times have come to East St. Louis is in evidence wherever you look. Of the few stores still operating near the center of town many have broken windows and peeling paint, rotting or missing trim, and few customers visible. The condition of the area is even more obvious when juxtaposed with the modern skyline of nearby downtown St. Louis, Missouri, easily seen from here. Recent years have seen an increased effort to develop, restore, and revitalize the East St. Louis community. Unfortunately buildings in many sections have begun to fall and will likely be too costly to restore and must eventually be razed to make room for newer structures.

Coming out of the remains of the downtown area the National Road heads north on a parallel to the Mississippi River, passing the local hospital and some industrial areas, before traveling under Interstate 55 and continuing west.

Above - The road surface of the National Road shows a great deal of deterioration and little maintenance through this residential section of East St. Louis, IL.

Below - The pattern of deterioration continues as we enter a business and industrial area of East St. Louis. The overgrowth of weeds, trash in the streets, and the numerous empty buildings make this area seem forgotten.

Passing under the Interstate immediately creates the sensation of having entered another world or country, the road is smooth and the area is clean and well lit.

The historic Eads Bridge spans the Mississippi River while a floating casino booat sits moored to the shore on the Illinois side of the river.

It takes but a short drive to understand the cause of the change. Here on the left side of the road we find the entrance to the recently renovated historic Eads Bridge (1874) with a new road surface creating a direct link to the modern city of St. Louis.

Ahead, our journey across the National Road ends beneath the Eads Bridge at the edge of the Mississippi River. Taking the time to turn left on the narrow road paralleling the river, a large well lit parking area can be seen and beyond it a riverboat casino is moored at shore. As we have seen before, at the Fairmount Racetrack Park near Collinsville, the casino and the age and make of many of the cars in the parking lot are a glaring contrast to the area of East St. Louis immediately behind it.

Continuing past the casino on this side road we can see an older ConAgra plant that is still in use to our left and to the right the levee with the railroad tracks running along the top. Along with the adjacent Mississippi River, the levee is symbolic of the former industrial life of the area and as a physical barrier between St. Louis and East St. Louis.

From this point we will backtrack past the casino to the entrance of the Eads Bridge. Parking nearby to the entrance ramp of the bridge and entering the pedestrian walkway we can travel from the base of the Eads Bridge across the Mississippi River and continue into the city of St. Louis, Missouri.

A short walk to the center of the bridge gives us an excellent view of the St. Louis Arch, the Old Courthouse, and the downtown area of the city of St. Louis, Missouri.

Above - Workboats pass each other while pushiing barges on the Mississippi River. Downtown St. Louis, MO and the Jefferson National Expansion Memorial are visible in the background.

Below - On specific weekends throughout the year the Eads Bridge is closed to vehicle traffic for special events. This car show took place during the statewide Illinois National Road Festival held onFather's Day weekend in June.

JEFFERSON NATIONAL EXPANSION MEMORIAL

Opposite us lies the city of St. Louis, Missouri and the Jefferson National Expansion Memorial more commonly referred to as the St. Louis Arch, a symbolic gateway celebrating the passage of early travelers to the western frontier and beyond.

Having traveled through six states and across many hundreds of miles we have now reached the end of our journey and the end of the National Road at the east bank of the Mississippi River.

THE END OF THE ROAD

For more information about the National Road and upcoming events or to join in the effort to preserve this important part of American History you can contact the following :

MARYLAND
Maryland National Road Association
P. O. Box 832
Ellicott City, Maryland 21041

PENNSYLVANIA
National Road Heritage Corridor
65 W Main Street, Second Floor
Uniontown, PA 15401
Phone   (724) 437-9877   email - info@nationalroadpa.org
Website   http://www.nationalroadpa.org/

WEST VIRGINIA
National Road Alliance of WV, Inc
P.O. Box 6338
Wheeling, WV 26003
Phone   304-312-3068 or 800-828-3097   email - info@historicwvnationalroad.org
Website   http://www.historicwvnationalroad.org/index.htm

OHIO
Ohio National Road Association
76 East High Street
Springfield, OH 45502
Phone   937-324-7752   email - lhimes@ci.springfield.oh.us

INDIANA
Indiana National Road Association
P.O. Box 284
Cambridge City, IN 47327
Phone   (765)478-3172   email - info@indiananationalroad.org
Website   http://www.indiananationalroad.org/

ILLINOIS
National Road Association of Illinois
800 East Industrial Drive
Toledo, Illinois 62468
Phone   888-268-0042 or 217-849-3188   Email: nationalrd@rr1.net
Website   www.nationalroad.org

RELATED RESOURCES
National Road / Zane Grey Museum
8850 East Pike
Norwich, OH 43767
Phone   740-872-3143 or 800-752-2602
Website   http://www.ohiohistory.org/places/natlroad/#info

Index